Grace for Shame

The Kingdom Solution for Reigning

Written By:

Mike Hillebrecht

Grace for Shame
The Kingdom Solution for Reigning

ISBN-13: 978-0615605500
ISBN-10: 0615605508

Unless noted otherwise all Scripture references are from the King
James Bible.

Due to the dynamic nature of the Internet, any website address or link
contained in this book may have changed and no longer may be valid.

More information may be obtained at www.graceforshame.com

Published by
Charis Academy Publishing
Portland, Oregon

www.charisacademy.org

Dedication

To my wife, Kari:
Googlepleck infinity

To Dr. Barry and Shawn Lenhardt:
Friends and mentors to the greatness which is within.

Contents

Preface

You have been exposed, stripped naked, left for the world to gawk at your blushing, twisted mass of quivering flesh. Your face, flushed red with embarrassment, anxiously scans for a place to retreat so your grotesque exposure will not be witnessed by those around you. Desperately you grasp for something — anything - to veil the humiliation of your circumstances. You have grabbed so many coverings that no one recognizes even who you are, including yourself, and you still scramble to find one more thing which will cover you and rid you of the embarrassment that you relive every single day. I'll stop here because you already know the effect shame has had upon your life. You, however, now hold in your hand the solution—yet it is up to you to determine if you're going to believe it.

Had you told me a year ago I would be writing about the subject of shame, I would have told you that you were nuts. I was buried in a study about grace and how it operates in the Kingdom of God. Shame had nothing to do with grace as far as I could see. Yet, one day, I was talking to a friend about a matter, and she spoke one word that sent me down a path which uncovered a treasure of untold riches. That one word was "disgrace," and it unveiled an aspect of grace on a plane I had never considered. What you hold in your hands is the treasure which I've uncovered.

When I began writing this, I had to determine who would be the audience I would be directing this towards—followers of Christ, commonly known as believers, or everyone else. After thinking about how to present the material to these two differing classes of people, I decided no matter what direction I would choose to take, it would be like nuts in a cinnamon roll. Some people like nuts and some don't. If you get a roll with nuts in it and you don't like them, the choices on your part are to pick out what you don't like; don't eat the roll; or eat it, enduring the minor inconvenience that the nuts make to your palate. I am writing this towards everyone who is in some way dealing with the nature and effect of shame.

Before you go forging ahead with the message, I want to clear up one thing: **I am not writing a religious message.** I say this because grace has been used by organizational moral leaders (i.e., religion) throughout history as a tool to capture those with a world view opposed to their message. While many of their intentions may have been worthy, often the actions they took produced a result completely opposite to the message. Unfortunately, this is explainable when you understand the original significance of the term "religion" found in the Latin language means "to bind or tie up again." Jesus, who is the representation of grace, came to set the captives free. This message is focused towards freedom, hence not religious.

You are about to venture into a world which is not like anything you have ever experienced. I can boldly proclaim this about the Kingdom of God because today many just don't understand how the kingdom operates, even though it was the only message that Jesus spoke about. Unfortunately, there is a slight dilemma to what you are about to read here that I'm willing to recognize right up front: You think you know what I'm going to talk about, so you'll probably only skim through this and see if there is anything "new" that you don't know. Let me explain.

In the book *The 21 Irrefutable Laws of Leadership* by John Maxwell, he states one of the laws in leadership is known as the "Law of the Lid." Simply put, this law suggests that every organization will only rise to the level of the person which leads it. If the leader is rated as a seven, the organization can only rise to the level of a six because the leader is the lid at the position of seven. This law even applies in a church environment! Have you ever been frustrated that the pastor doesn't ever get to the "meat" of the matter in a service? He is dealing with the lid, but it's not one that he controls. This lid is what I call the Mrs. Jones Effect.

Our brains are wonderfully and marvelously made to take in a variety of information through numerous receptors in our bodies. As we process this information, we begin to recognize patterns in events and begin creating catalogues of these patterns as a way of being able to efficiently work with all the information. Some of these catalogues of patterns become our beliefs, and over time, they have become so ingrained that when we even begin to see the first occurrence of a pattern, we instantly acknowledge it resembles a particular catalogue and subsequently activates our "long-held" belief. So why do I call this the Mrs. Jones Effect?

If you were raised in a church environment from a child, you probably had a Mrs. Jones in the child ministry. Her ministry gift was her ability to keep a class of small children quiet and occupied during the 45 minutes that the adult service lasted. Any spiritual lessons provided were designed to be simple in context so they could be accomplished in the time frame dictated by the length of the grown-up message. These lessons (i.e., The Fall of Man, Noah and the Flood, Samson, David and Goliath, Jesus Walks on the Water, and of course the Christmas/Easter stories) were repeated frequently during the child's formative years. From these lessons, we developed our spiritual catalogue of beliefs. Regrettably, these lessons have become your lid!

Now I understand that some of you may never have been raised in this type of environment. You came to Christ as an adult, so the Mrs. Jones Effect can't apply to you, right? Consider this: Is the person instructing you in your congregation a past student of Mrs. Jones?[1] This is the lid which your pastor has to deal with weekly. Some beliefs are just plain stuck in Mrs. Jones' class, and he can only present certain truths a little at a time, since it is so difficult to pull the lid off of what Mrs. Jones has created.

So I trust that you now realize my dilemma in presenting this material to you. You have a belief in what the topic is about. This belief is not right or wrong; it is your belief. My question to you is this: Are you willing to take the lid off of your belief and question why you believe what you believe? Are you willing to look at your belief in a whole new manner which can make you more empowered?

---

[1] Mrs. Jones is a fictional character that I have created to demonstrate a point. If your name is Mrs. Jones and you work in child ministry, I have the greatest respect for you and your gift. I trust that you will be able to recognize my point in this matter and understand that the lessons that you present to our children are a vital component to developing a strong spiritual character.

It will be my purpose on the following pages to convey an aspect of grace to you which will enable you to break off the shackles that have held you back from fulfilling the destiny which God has created you to have. While space does not permit me to convey everything about grace that I have found and continue to daily uncover, I will instill the foundational essence which will subsequently permit me to address the nature of shame and how grace deals with it. Some of this material will come directly from either the book's website, www.graceforshame.com, or www.mygrace2u.com, both of which I contribute towards, while other parts will be fresh from the oven, so to speak. It is not my intent to regurgitate someone else's material here but show you what has been shown to me and, if need be, use other material as a springboard into the revelation.

Those who know me call me "Teacher." That, I believe, is the grace-gift given to me long before I was "saved." You will find employed in the following pages techniques which can only come from one who enjoys teaching others. I enjoy knowing what a word truly means in all of its various forms, but I don't like to be bogged down in the "intellectual pursuit" of knowing just to know. I also want to understand why someone says something the way they do, so historical matters and social customs help me to comprehend this. These two tools are the underpinning of the "how and why" I write the way I do. Someone once said that every truly great writer writes for an audience of one: themselves. So in these pages which I write for myself, I trust you will gain the insight to help make your life all God intended it to be.

Hebrews 4:12 tells us God's word is living today just as it was when it was spoken and written down so many years ago. For those of you, who get hung up on the word tense used in a manuscript, relax. If something is still living, its presence is present today. This was the choice I made throughout this work. It's not about what God did; it's about what He is still doing with the same words.

I would be greatly remiss as someone who understands the basis of grace if I did not take time to acknowledge with sincere thanks those working behind the scenes that have made this effort possible. To my wife who has taken on so much over our relationship, I greatly appreciate and love you. Thanks must go to Dr. Barry Lenhardt and his wife, Shawn, who have been great friends, role models and spiritual mentors. It is the environment of heaven you've created and maintained at ILC which has birthed much of this material. Shawn, I greatly appreciate your diligent review of the manuscript and the kingdom conversations that it produced between us. Thank you to the prayer network that has covered me over the past several months while I have been working on this. Your prayers have been felt and deeply appreciated. A special thanks to Sarajoy Bonebright who helped to edit the manuscript. Finally, to those who I haven't directly mentioned— you know who you are—thanks so much for your support and love. I am a blessed man to have such a good group of friends.

My prayer is that the eyes of your heart be opened and that the Spirit of God would move over the words which are before you and bring newness of life into your being. I ask that a healing balm be administered where it is needed and that a fierce determination to reside in the abundant life of the Kingdom of God be birthed in you. Finally, may God receive all the glory which is due Him through the life-altering change you are about to experience.

Grace and Peace to You,

Mike

Part 1
Grace

Once an identity begins to take root in our lives, it becomes self-perpetuating and reinforces itself. This is true across the board — cities, regions or people, kingdom or demonic — it is a principle of "life."

Paul Manwaring
Bethel Church
Redding, Ca

1.1 What is Grace?

For God pays no attention to this world's distinctions... For when Gentiles who have no Law obey by natural instinct the commands of the Law, they, without having a Law, are a Law to themselves; since they exhibit proof that a knowledge of the conduct which the Law requires is engraven on their hearts, while their consciences also bear witness to the Law, and their thoughts, as if in mutual discussion, accuse them or perhaps maintain their innocence—on the day when God will judge the secrets of men's lives by Jesus Christ, as declared in the Good News as I have taught it. – Romans 2:11, 14-16

Does it strike you as kind of odd that the opening passage about the subject of grace doesn't mention it at all? You might think that if I was to impress upon you the importance of this matter, then I should at least make an impact with a "grace" scripture which will define the entire context of this subject. So let me make any impact in a different manner: Are you a sinner saved by grace, or a son sitting next to the throne of grace? How you answer this question determines how you operate daily in the nature which is known as grace.

I want to bring an understanding to the message of grace as viewed from the perspective of the Kingdom of God and not as it applies to the fall of man. Almost every believer knows they have been saved by grace, but after that, then what is grace for?

This opening passage of Scripture describes what happens when a concept embodied in a social order has the ability to appear as a divine portrayal of the Kingdom of God. Paul is conveying to believers that sometimes we will see someone who we know is not a believer act in a fashion which is purely from God's Word, even though they don't realize it themselves. This is what Paul calls "natural instinct." Grace is a natural instinct with many kingdom implications.

Most of us have used the term "grace" in one capacity or another when we attempt to describe a visible attribute which we're impressed by. We say ballet dancers are graceful in their movements or that Fred Astaire had a certain grace about him when he walked into a room. Most religious people will say grace before a meal as a means of staying in the good grace of God. There are those who see a horse running and are in awe of the grace in which they pass other horses on the way to the finish line. Some are drawn to the graceful curves of a new automobile, just as others are drawn to the graceful moves of a cheetah chasing an antelope. Most of us have been entertained by the gracious host or hostess or have left a gratuity for someone who has served us exceptionally well. We even know intuitively when we are not in the good graces of a spouse, friend or co-worker, just as we know when we have been graced by someone in our lives. Sure, I'm even grateful that you have decided to read this material! But do any of these examples bring you to an understanding of the term "grace"?

For our purpose here, I'm going to define grace as an enabling factor that permits you to accomplish a predetermined task, role or function. This definition covers divine and natural grace; the difference being divine grace is unconditional while natural grace is not.

I recognize that I will receive a lot of flack from people who will take an exception to my definition being too simplistic or not "theologically" sound enough (whatever that means). Don't bother emailing me about it. I just acknowledged your ability to have a grievance, and you are forgiven (a concept you'll learn about in a few chapters). So welcome to a real study of grace as it was meant to be: seen from the view of the Kingdom of God as described in the New Testament.

The New Testament word which we read as grace is the Greek word "charis" (pronounced "Khar'-ece"), and its rich history in the Greek culture predates the New Testament writings by over 600 years. Its concepts cannot easily be boiled down to one or two simple words or sentences which will properly portray the vast richness and complexities that this single word spans. Yet still we must begin somewhere in trying to convey the underlying essence of this word.

The entire New Testament writings are filled with the word "charis". It occurs 156 times as twelve different words in the King James Version of the Bible. Throughout much of church history, we have assigned a meaning to this word which has lost much of its original character—not that this is bad, it's just not a complete picture. I want you to get re-acquainted with the word from the understanding of the early Greek poets as they used it in their writings. I hope to show how the Greeks viewed the importance of this word in their daily lives and how it corresponds to passages in the Bible.

What is unique about *"charis"* is that Paul in his writings took this one word and single-handedly redefined it (not in a bad sense), elevating it to an entirely new level of meaning. Today, we don't even recognize this and subsequently miss out on the deeper meaning of the text when we read it. I hope to be able to provide you with not only an introduction to the Greek understanding of this word but also to know how this will affect your interpretation of very common Bible passages.

When is the beginning?

Let me ask you a question. Do you know when grace began?

Most people have never thought about it. Why should you? After all, you're saved by grace. You've got your "Get into Heaven Free Card."

Is it possible that there could be something more important to the nature of grace than getting into heaven? If the question has been asked, it's possible that looking into this matter may have ramifications upon your walk as a Christian.

So when do you think it began? Was it when you accepted Jesus as Lord of your life? Or was it at His sacrifice on the cross? Or maybe it was in the garden of Gethsemane when He proclaimed "...not my will but Your will be done." How about when He was born? With so many choices, it's becoming evident that the beginning of grace could have a different impact on your life depending on where you view it. Fortunately, the Bible has the answer for us.

Who hath saved us, and called us with a holy calling, not
*according to our works, but according to his own purpose **and***
grace**, which was given us in Christ Jesus **before the world
***began**. – 2 Timothy 1:9*

There is the answer, and it probably is not what you were expecting, right? When anything is defined as "before the world began," you're talking about something which comes from an eternal realm. This means grace is not trafficking in time, or in other words, there is, and was, never a time when grace did not exist. So even when you consider the times listed above, grace was in operation—even at the creation of the world! This means that when the man and the woman fell, grace was operating. But can you spot it working?

> GRACE IS OUT OF THE DOMAIN OF CAUSE AND EFFECT BECAUSE IT IS AN ETERNAL COMPONENT. GRACE WAS PRESENT BEFORE ANY CAUSE.

Probably not, since *charis*, or grace as you know it, is a Greek term. You won't find a Greek word in a book originally written in Hebrew. But if you know what the characteristics of *charis* are from a New Testament Greek perspective, then you'll be able to recognize it in the Old Testament Hebrew writings.

There is a kingdom.

There are a number of things Paul conveys in this one passage from 2 Timothy 1:9 that relate to the kingdom, but for now, I just want you to focus on the component of grace here. Throughout this writing, you will come across a term I use quite frequently. It is "Kingdom of Grace." Not many people have every heard this, and I believe this is due to a lack of understanding the operation of God's Kingdom as described in the Bible. As you read further along, you will see for yourself the simplicity in this term to illustrate a very complex subject.

If you're going to begin any discussion on God's Kingdom, then we have to begin at the required kingdom Scripture of Matthew 6:33, which says the following:

> But seek **_first the kingdom of God and His righteousness_**, and all these things shall be added to you."

Jesus is pretty clear about what is important here in this verse. So let me ask you something: When you think about what a kingdom looks like, what do you envision? Is it dominion, lands, castles, wealth, abundance? That's good, but it's not complete yet. Certainly, every kingdom has a king, and he wears a crown. Land comes with being a king. Yes, there are housing obligations which come with being a king, and there certainly is all that abundance which the territory produces on behalf of the king. However, there is one item every kingdom has which most people overlook:

> "Let us therefore come boldly to the **_throne of grace_**, that we may obtain mercy and find **_grace_** to help in time of need." – Hebrews 4:16

A throne is the point where all power and authority is administrated by a king. It identifies the nature and realm of the king. In Isaiah, we are told the Messiah will rule from the throne of David. Here in the book of Hebrews, we are told to go boldly to the Throne of Grace, and when we do that, we are able to obtain mercy and find grace. Mercy and grace have always been viewed from the perspective of a fallen man. But let me tell you that they have nothing to do with the fall since both were present before the foundation of the world. If the truth be told (and why shouldn't it?), in many ways, they represent the same thing in the Kingdom of God: One is a concept unique to the Hebrews, and the other is unique to the Greeks. Together they explain the relationship of a king to his creation as He intended it to be.

If you know anything about how a kingdom operates, no one can boldly approach a throne unless they have been declared by the king to be in "right standing" with him. The official term is "righteous." Now we get to round out the picture from the verse in Matthew as we recognize that the kingdom operates from a throne of grace which we can boldly go before because we're righteous. What's that? You don't know about this righteous part?

For He made Him who knew no sin to be sin for us, that we might become the righteousness of God in Him. – 2 Corinthians 5:21

There, God took care of that for you too. If you're in Jesus, then you have God's righteousness, and that's pretty important to Him. In order for grace to operate, you, I, anybody for that matter, have to have righteousness. This has been your introduction to the Kingdom of Grace. It has always been there. You just didn't recognize it!

The Pleasure Factor

When I speak about grace to most people, there is this very somber mood which comes upon them as they relate to me their experiences of how grace has touched or affected their lives. At first, I took this reverent tone as a mannerism of their experience, but recently, I've become aware that this may be not the case. It is

---

possible that the response is simply ignorance about the true nature of grace and what it produces. Before you go and get your dander up, let me explain.

Grace, like most words, has a root word which it comes from. Root words are foundational in understanding the meaning of not only a word but how its use can be interpreted in its context. If you know the root, you know how to properly advance the meaning of the word.

The Greek word we know as grace is, as I've stated, *charis*. This word comes from the root word *"chara."* You'll discover *chara's* meaning in this passage of Scripture:

*For the kingdom of God is not meat and drink; but righteousness, and peace, and **joy** (chara) in the Holy Ghost. – Romans 14:17*

"*Chara*" is defined as 1) joy, gladness; 1a) the joy received from you; 1b) the cause or occasion of joy; 1b1) of persons who are one's joy. The interesting aspect of this word is that it too has a root word which it comes from. "*Chara*" comes from the word "*chairo*," which is defined as 1) to rejoice, be glad; 2) to rejoice exceedingly; 3) to be well, thrive; 4) in salutations, hail!; 5) at the beginning of letters: to give one greeting, salute. This word, "*chairo*," can be found in this passage:

<u>Rejoice</u> (chairo) in the Lord always; and again, I say, <u>Rejoice</u> (chairo). – Philippians 4:4

So what does all of this mean? Well, any discussion about grace has to take into consideration the fact that whatever the meaning of grace is, its very foundation is built upon the nature of joy and rejoicing. This means that there is a nature of pleasure associated with whatever grace means, and this pleasure is expressive in a positive manner.

So why the frowns and sullen expressions whenever the matter of grace arises? As I said, it's ignorance about the basic nature of grace. Most congregants have been indoctrinated that God stands over them with a bat and waits to clobber them at any moment they make the slightest mistake. This mindset is then filtered out into the "world" through our daily discourse so even our relationships with the "world" are tainted.

THE DIFFERENCE BETWEEN THE PASSAGE IN MATTHEW 6:33 AND LUKE 12:31 HAS TO DO WITH WHO THE WRITER IS TALKING TO. MATTHEW IS ADDRESSED TO THE HEBREWS AND LUKE IS ADDRESSED TO THE GREEKS.

Consider that when you begin to smile, you may actually be moving into the realm of grace more than you realize. The Old Testament clearly states that, "...Joy of the Lord is your strength." So we can say that the foundation of grace, which is joy, is your strength. And so where is this leading us? It's leading us to Luke's interpretation of Matthew 6:33.

*But rather seek ye the kingdom of God; and all these things shall be added unto you. Fear not, little flock; **for it is your Father's good pleasure** to give you the kingdom. – Luke 12:31-32*

It's time to now go a little deeper and explore a few of the many facets which enabled the New Testament writers to communicate with a culture who understood the fullness of grace as it resided on the earth during their day. Yes, that statement implies there are at least two types of grace: the grace of man and the grace of the Kingdom of God. Many don't understand this and think that there is only one. Unfortunately, you can't live in the Kingdom of God employing the grace of man. My purpose from this point forward will be to point out to you the differences between the two so you'll be able to align yourself correctly.

Make a note to yourself: **If a distinction is not made, it applies to both equally.**

Reciprocal Grace

And as you would that men should do to you, do you also to them likewise. – Luke 6:31

The Golden Rule is something as children many are required to memorize. It is basic sandbox etiquette that mothers have tried to instill in their children for centuries.   Many people can tell you what the Golden Rule is, but they are hard pressed to be able to tell you where to find it in the Bible. These verses in the Gospel of Luke and also one located at Matthew 7:12 are what we know to be the Golden Rule. So what does it have to do with grace, since the very word isn't even used in either verse?

*...**for this is the characteristic of grace**—we should serve in return one who has shown grace to us, and should another time take the initiative in showing it. – Nicomachean Ethics, Book V, Aristotle*

Some 300 plus years before Jesus uttered the words recorded in Matthew and Luke, Aristotle had defined the characteristic of grace.

Now this might offend some people because they don't think that anything which came out of a "pagan" culture could have something remotely associated with a biblical truth.

I respect your rights to deal with this material in any manner you desire, but I want you to consider this before we proceed: Of the 27 books canonized in the New Testament, eight are written to church congregants who could trace their ancestry back to the time of Aristotle; two books are written to an influential Greek benefactor who also could possibly trace his heritage back to Aristotle; three books are written to overseers of churches located in this same region and describe how drawing on the cultural history will impact the new believer; and one book was written to church congregants that had deposed the Greek empire, integrated its population, and become the ruling empire of the age. This means that over 50% of the New Testament was addressing the Greeks and not in word form only. A simple reading of Luke's account of Paul's journeys in the book of Acts clearly indicates that, in many cases, it wasn't the Jews who welcomed the gospel message but the Greeks. This is why I have proceeded down this path. I have nothing against the Jews and their culture; after all, they gave us the Messiah. In order to understand the importance of grace, we have to come at it from the Greek culture where its very operation was already ingrained in the societal structure.

Knowing what we do about what Paul preached, what about it was so influential to a pagan culture that it eventually took over the entire region? It's simple: Paul spoke about grace which came from Heaven in the form of Jesus. It wasn't a Jewish Messiah that these listeners heard about; it was about the reciprocal nature of grace in the exchange which Jesus made for them. They lived this reciprocal lifestyle in their community; their poets and philosophers had written about this nature of grace for centuries. Now, they were hearing how God was interacting with them on the same basis. Their own gods never conducted themselves in this manner—even the *Charites* who were known as "The Three Graces" never operated in this fashion! And now hearing this, they experienced the foundational component of grace: joy.

We have lost this understanding today, much to the disadvantage of new believers. There is much more to this characteristic of grace that we'll be exploring in the study ahead of us, but I want this to be the point of demarcation where what you've thought you knew about grace could possibly be incomplete.

1.2 Charis – Fact or Fiction

In the opening pages of 1 Samuel, we read the story of the two wives of Elkanah. Peninnah, the first wife, inflicted mental abuse upon Hannah, the second wife, since she was unable to bear a child. If you've done any Bible study, you know Hannah has a child, named Samuel, who eventually becomes the one who anoints David, Israel's greatest king, the forerunner to Jesus the Messiah. What, you may ask, does all of this have to do with *charis*?

I use this well known story as measuring tool in time because at the same time, several hundred miles to the north, on the northwestern edge of present day Turkey, a war is being fought, one which would last for ten years—a war that would become the defining moment for all of the Greek culture. This war would shape the character of national leaders, like Alexander the Great, who was to come almost 800 years after the battle had been fought. This war would be analyzed by great writers, poets, philosophers and military strategists for centuries, even up to this day. If the Red Sea was the defining moment for the tribe of Israel, this war, the Trojan War, was such a moment for Greece. Embodied within the backdrop of this conflict are the beginnings of what we know of the nature of *charis*.

After this great war, just as many before had run their course, champions and vanquished each went their way, telling the stories of great battles and their heroes to any who would listen. And since they didn't have our modern conveniences of communication, weekly, if not nightly, symposiums, which were the mainstay of the communal life, became the outlet for these stories. Symposiums, unlike today's dry, staid intellectual forums, were in those days festive drinking events held after a communal feast, where songs and stories of heroic deeds from the champions of the past and the present flowed as easily as the wine, which by its very nature, was the regulator on the ability of the teller to hold the attention of the audience.

Over and over again, these grand and noble stories would be told, each generation adding to their richness, as new subjects of honor arose in the community. This is what we might call the oral traditions of a culture, but to them, it was an element of *charis*— giving honor to those who honor was due. *Charis*, in this public venue, was something every man acknowledged as important to the fabric of the community. *Charis* constrained their affairs so they would not to be seen operating without honor, which could be brought up in these public events just as well.

One of the oldest pieces of Greek literature, penned by Homer, is called *The Iliad*. Homer wrote about the Trojan War over two hundred years after the events transpired, at about the time that Solomon was dedicating the Temple of God in 1 Kings 7. Why is this important? The narrative of this ten year war was not penned by someone that witnessed it firsthand but by someone, who understanding the first nature of *charis*, was willing to bring honor where honor was due to as many as would receive it.

While much of the Homer's text describes the battles which led to the fall of the city where Helen of Troy had been held captive, its underlying theme revolves around a famous champion named Achilles and the abuse of *charis* towards him by his commander. This transgression leads to many critical developments throughout the story which reveal the varied nature of *charis* and its import in the daily lives of the people in those times.

Some 600 years after Homer describes the *charis* of Achilles in *The Iliad*, Aristotle declares the distinguishing characteristic of *charis* is reciprocity in the *Nicomachean Ethics, Book 5*. Today, we would know this reciprocal process as The Golden Rule: Do unto others as you would have them do unto you. But how could this Greek society operate under such a clearly "biblical" order?

Consider that Greece, now as then, is comprised of a main land and many islands, which "in the day" were primarily agricultural. Each of these islands were inhabited by clans which were fiercely independent yet socially dependent upon each other. Whenever a conflict would arise, which could draw the men capable of fighting away from their homes, as a matter of social discourse, those who remained behind would tend to the estates of those who had gone on their behalf. This would create a bond within the societal order to insure the protection of the community, not only in the present circumstance but also for future conflicts that might arise. Future generations were expected to fulfill their duty in honoring the sacrifices of those who had gone before them as an obligation to their own family's commitment to protect the interests of a neighbor.

This honoring of the obligations, or a *"charis*-event," would be the glue which held the Greek society together for so many centuries. Some scholars even speculate that the reason that

Greece never rose to a great economic power in the world was because of the rule of *charis* even in their business dealings.

Mankind has always felt the obligation to return a gift or favor from someone who is close to them or in a position where they might have an influence in their life, like a boss, business associate, politician or the like. During this time, and even up until the Apostle Paul, the Greek culture was structured such that in order to obtain any position of influence, it was expected for one to give or work towards the favor of a benefactor who could place them into the position which was being sought. This process of obtaining favor from a benefactor was known during this time period as "*charis*"—the very word which is transcribed as "grace" in the New Testament. Understanding this concept now, you may be able to understand what Paul is stating in this passage.

> For **by grace** you have been saved through faith, and that not of yourselves; it is the **gift of God, not of works**, lest anyone should boast. – Ephesians 2:8-9

Here Paul is letting the people of Ephesus know that the nature of grace which saves them is the nature that *charis* really had so many years prior to Aristotle, when the social structure of reciprocal giving was conducted as a means of ensuring the survival of the community when danger was present.

The important factor in this transaction was that no one was compelled to return the favor immediately. It was understood that this form of grace was generational in nature, meaning the return of the favor may not be needed to be returned until the next threat appeared, which might not happen for several decades or even a lifetime. This original definition of *charis* (grace) is what Paul is re-establishing with the church at Ephesus so they could see the kingdom of God operates in a manner which they may be familiar within their family structures.

What, you might ask, would happen if *charis* was not honored? In a societal structure so tightly interdependent upon one another, not honoring the *charis* which was extended to you by a neighbor was grounds for public humiliation and disgrace. It was acceptable practice to "call out" the offending party at any public gathering so as to insure the community would be fully aware of the nature of the individual and how they conducted themselves with regards to commitments. In small

> WHEN *CHARIS* WAS NOT RETURNED BY ONE PARTY IT WAS CUSTOM TO CALL THE OFFENDING PARTY OUT IN PUBLIC. THIS IS THE BASIS OF DISGRACE OR WHAT IS MORE COMMONLY KNOWN AS SHAME.

communities, this would be devastating to the person and their family for many generations afterwards, since it would adversely affect their daily transactions within the community as well as virtually deprive them of any ability to protect their resources in any future conflict. This communal disgrace they experienced is more commonly known as shame.

So we see here that *charis* has a specific nature associated with it which is evident in the actions of reciprocal exchange. This exchange process created a mechanism of honor which was passed down from generation to generation as reciprocal exchanges occurred within the social and economic fabric of each community. Eventually, this pattern would become tarnished in the larger urban areas through the mechanism of political advantage and the buying of "favors" to extend and secure one's influence in the community. Yet in the rural areas, the operation of *charis,* as it first developed, would remain the law of the land.

This heritage of reciprocity in the context of *charis*, or grace, is what Paul and Luke would draw upon in their dialogues with the churches in their day. In today's language, we don't use the term "reciprocal" much to explain social discourse. If you wanted to get into a more relevant term that portrayed the transaction between the parties, we could use "exchange." But our most frequently used term which conveys the appropriate symbolism is primarily "give" or "gave."

Recall that the root meaning of grace is joy, so tying this together with reciprocity, we should see that grace is joyful giving. This is a concept which is pretty transparent even in our daily lives. Who doesn't get joy from giving a gift? Obviously, we often enjoy receiving them more than giving them, but that aside, the pleasure which comes from the transaction of giving is what the early Greeks recognized as an operation of grace. If this is true, then it should show up in Scripture in other locations also. Well, here are a few of the more memorable verses.

> *Every man according as he purposeth in his heart, so let him give; not grudgingly, or of necessity: for God loveth a cheerful giver. – 2 Corinthians 9:7*

For God so loved the world, that he gave his only begotten Son, that whosoever believeth in him should not perish, but have everlasting life. – John 3:16

Having predestinated us unto the adoption of children by Jesus Christ to himself, according to the good pleasure of his will..."
– Ephesians 1:5

Having made known unto us the mystery of his will, according to his good pleasure which he hath purposed in himself...
– Ephesians 1:9

In these passages, we see that there is a nature of pleasure the Father demonstrates in His activities with us. This is a result of the dimension of grace which surrounds and emanates from His throne. Don't get me wrong here: The Father is not demonstrating pleasure simply from a position of authority. This would be like saying that you're only pleased with your kids when you can control what their interaction is with you. Pleasure is as fundamental with the nature of the Father as it is with us: He has made it a visible component of His realm, and His purposes reflect it. This even applies where we least expect it.

*Yet it **pleased** the LORD to bruise him; he hath put him to grief: when thou shalt make his soul an offering for sin, he shall see his seed, he shall prolong his days, and the **pleasure** of the LORD shall prosper in his hand. – Isaiah 53:10*

The Hebrew term of grace is vastly different from the Greeks, and yet, Isaiah is speaking of events which would occur when the ruling powers of the region would be operating with Greek understanding. Isaiah's language would then reflect what he was seeing prophetically. Even a casual reader of the Bible has difficulty with this passage when you speak of pleasure being derived from beating someone. However, understanding that this pleasure is coming from a realm where the authority and judgments made are based upon a purpose which pleases the sovereign in a reciprocal manner, then this difficulty is overcome. The transaction, or exchange, conducted in this verse by the bruising, returns a prosperous, prolonging of days that pleases the Lord.

So now understanding this matter of the pleasure of grace, its reciprocal nature, and the joy in giving, let's look at this verse:

> *I have shewed you all things, how that so labouring ye ought to support the weak, and to remember the words of the Lord Jesus, how he said, "**It is more blessed to give than to receive.**" – Acts 20:35*

In this passage, Paul is relaying to leaders from the church of Ephesus a revelation he received from the Lord. This portion which I have highlighted is a direct quote from the Lord, and if you own a red-letter Bible, it will be in red. It does not appear in any of the gospels, making this a vital saying of the Lord in our discussion. Notice that grace is not mentioned, but now knowing about the nature of grace, I trust that you can see how this statement naturally embodies it. Yet, even here, we need to look a little deeper.

Deeper Grace

> *Who hath saved us, and called us with a holy calling, not according to our works, but according to **his own purpose and grace**, which was given us in Christ Jesus **before the world began**... – 2 Timothy 1:9*

We're going to take another look at the beginnings. This won't be the last time we visit this subject, since everything we're delving into starts here (go figure!). I introduced the above verse previously when discussing what you thought about when grace began. "Before the world began..." is the important part of our entire discussion on grace, since it gives us a means of determining "time." The difficulty is that time, as we know it, is defined to a creation event noted in Genesis 1:14:

And God said, Let there be lights in the firmament of the heaven to divide the day from the night; and let them be for signs, and for seasons, and for days, and years...

So what is time called prior to Genesis 1:14? Eternity. We see in the first thirteen verses of Genesis the works which are being conducted in the eternal realm, and according to 2 Timothy 1:9, grace is an eternal component of God's purpose. What does this mean to us? Let's take a look at this from a salvation perspective.

According to the traditional salvation message a point occurs where you make the decision to accept the lordship of Jesus over your life. This point is defined by recognition of your sin against God and the only remedy is found in the work which Jesus accomplished for you. It is possible that you may have heard a message which made reference the term "saved by grace," which comes from Ephesians 2:4-5:

*But God, who is rich in mercy, for his great love wherewith he loved us, even when we were dead in sins, hath quickened us together with Christ, **by grace ye are saved...***

Most people believe that their salvation follows a "cause and effect" mechanism: My sin (cause) separates me from God (effect); I accept Jesus (cause) and regain access to God (effect). The dilemma with this thinking is most people who prolong their salvation decision do so because they don't believe they have done anything in their life up to the salvation moment which can be viewed as "sin." In other words, they are looking for a "time" in their life when they committed something wrong (cause) which would require them to turn to Jesus (effect). **Cause and effect mechanisms are bound in time events.**

Do you understand what I just said? Every effect is the result over a span of time from some cause. Everything which occurs in a dimension of time is a result of something that transpired prior to the event in the same time dimension. Dimensions of time have a starting point (cause) and an ending point (effect). Life on this planet is one big cause and effect scenario being played out with billions of people. **Yet grace isn't a component of this time dimension—it is eternal.** This means that your salvation "by grace" is not based upon any previous time event (cause). But we are time-based creatures, right? How can salvation not be a "cause and effect" mechanism? The answer is found in Romans 6:23:

> For the wages of sin is death; but **the _gift_ of God is eternal life** through Jesus Christ our Lord.

Death, you've got to admit, is a time-based element. We call the beginning of something bound in time as the "birth," while the end of the same thing as "death." So let me ask you ask a couple of questions: 1) Have you died in Christ? 2) Are you born again? Notice in both of these "salvation" questions a reference is made to a time-event in the words "died" and "born." What does this have to do with Romans 6:23?

The gift of God is "eternal" life. The gift is not bound by time. There is no beginning or end of the gift. The time-dimensional characteristic of eternity is that it is always "now." The gift of eternal life is always now. Get ready for this: The word "gift" in this verse has the root meaning of "grace." The "grace-gift" from God is eternal life. Breaking this down further with what you now know from our previous notes: **The joyous, grace-gift reciprocally given of God is a life which constantly keeps you "now" and is not bound by the cause and effect mechanism of time.** Your salvation is an ending of a life bound in time and a new-birth into an eternal realm where there is no death. This is your grace-gift from God: a life like His.

1.3 Abounding in Grace

*The thief cometh not, but for to steal, and to kill, and to destroy: I am come that they might have **life**, and that they might have it **more abundantly**. – John 10:10*

I trust you're developing a better awareness to the nature of grace, because here is another facet of grace which must not be overlooked. In our verse above, Jesus declares this very nature that we'll look at next: Grace abounds.

Jesus said that the thief comes to steal, kill and destroy. It is a three-pronged attack which the enemy will employ against every person on this planet. Have you had anything stolen from you? I'll deal with the death issue in a moment. How about having something destroyed? We've all had these things happen to us more than once in our lives. Many are still dealing with the bitter memories of these attacks and the impact they have had on their destiny. (What's interesting is that most insurance companies have an exclusion in their policies which they call "An Act of God" which protects them in the event of catastrophic events. They clearly don't know the difference between an act of God and that of the thief!)

Jesus says that He has come "that they might have..." This phrase is one Greek word in both of its occurrences here in this passage. It is the Greek word "echo," the same word that we get the present day word "echo." Now you know what an echo is, don't you? Yep, a **reciprocal** sound effect. The unique property of an echo is that it replicates an original; it doesn't do anything different on its own accord. Also, an echo will dissipate over a period of time, but Jesus said that it will "more abound," which in the Greek is a violent, excessive, uncommon abundance. This means that you are to have a life which expresses a previously spoken word and continue having an expression of this spoken word in a super-overwhelming fashion without end.

Recall that the joyous, grace-gift of God reciprocally given to you is a life like His. Jesus validates this claim, stating that He came to give us what the Greek's call "*zōē*" life. *Vine's Expository Dictionary* defines this Greek word for life as:

> THE PRIMARY NATURE OF THE KINGDOM OF GOD IS LIFE. THERE IS NO DEATH ANYWHERE IN ITS REALM. THIS LIFE IS ETERNAL, EVERLASTING. IT GOES ON FOREVER. THEN WHY ARE PEOPLE TRYING SO HARD TO GET TO HEAVEN?

Life as a principle, life in the absolute sense, life as God has it, that which the Father has in Himself, and which He gave to the Incarnate Son to have in Himself, and which the Son manifested in the world.

The primary nature of the Kingdom of God is Life. There is no death anywhere in its realm. This life is eternal, everlasting. It goes on forever. There is not a single person who would deny this very aspect of the Kingdom of God. This is why so many desire to go to heaven so they may have this life in them. Yet consider that Jesus came to give this life to you here on this earth, now. The fact that so many can't seem to grasp this truth is, well, unbelievable. Our inability to accept a truth does not change its nature; it only changes our direction away from the truth. Consider this quote from Jesus:

...making the word of God of no effect through your tradition which you have handed down. And many such things you do.
– Mark 7:13

If you've read the Genesis account of the fall of man, you know God said that in the day man ate the fruit from the tree of the knowledge of good and evil that he would die. Well he ate it, and he didn't die that day—at least not in the sense we know of it. It took over 900 years for the first man to learn how to die. We have so perfected this knowledge it only now takes most people 60 to 70 years to accomplish the same results. A handed down tradition of death is more accepted to society than the Word of God which clearly proclaims life.

"But they died!" is what I'm hearing from you. I'm not being callous or heartless here. I too have experienced the pain which comes from death. So let's take a moment to consider this: Do you believe that they are in Heaven, in the Kingdom of God? Do you agree there is no death in that realm? Their earth suit may have retired, but their spirit certainly didn't. They presently reside in a realm of such abounding grace that they wish you knew about it. There is an entire host in Heaven which is cheering over this message you are reading. They want all of us to finally embrace this truth and begin to live it out here on the earth. Okay, let's get back to this matter of abundance.

If man had not sinned in the Garden of Eden, would he have died? If Jesus had not given His life, would He still be here today?

These are not trick questions. They are foundational questions in understanding how grace operates because they both address the abundant nature of an eternal life.

Does it abound?

*Moreover the law entered, that the offense might abound. But where sin abounded, **grace did much more abound:** That as sin hath reigned unto death, even so might grace reign through righteousness unto **eternal life** by Jesus Christ our Lord.*
– Romans 5:20-21

How much does grace abound? This was revealed to me one day when I was putting away the clean dishes. I picked up a teaspoon to place it in the drawer, and I heard the Spirit of God say to me, "This is the amount of sin that abounded." Dumbfounded, all I could respond with was, "Okay." Immediately, I saw a picture of the Pacific Ocean like you would see on a map, and the Spirit said, "This is grace that abounds."

This passage in Romans 5 is a whole grace study in itself, which I don't have space to develop fully, so I want to focus on this one point: Why does grace abound more than sin? Consider this: Some scientists say that, today, the entire population of this planet exceeds all of the people who have ever lived on the planet previously. Life abounds more than death. I don't know if you realize this, but death, and anything which resembles or leads to it, doesn't have a way of reproducing itself like life does. Life has the ability to create

THE ABOUNDING
MEASUREMENT OF
GRACE

SIN = 1 TEASPOON

GRACE = PACIFIC OCEAN

something called "generations," which echo the original pattern. Death is a one-trick pony, while life is an entire circus.

Why does grace abound? It honors life. How did I arrive at such a conclusion? Grace reigns through righteousness unto eternal life. "Reign" is a word which indicates a position of supreme authority and encompasses the honor the position represents. "Righteousness" means right-standing, correct, according to right thinking. So let's assemble this together: **Joyous, reciprocal giving operates correctly from a position of preeminence which controls the environment of an eternal, everlasting life.** This is why grace abounds; this is what you have been saved into; this is your heritage, and how you express it on this earth is your destiny in Christ Jesus.

Are you beginning to see the importance of grace from the perspective of the King? Then why have we allowed ourselves to live as paupers on this earth when it is not the intent of the King? Whose echo are you resounding?

1.4 Grace is not . . .

Prepare yourself. I'm going to slay a religious cow.

In this journey through the understanding of grace, I have tried to show you that the nature of grace is multi-faceted—one aspect cannot properly define it completely. I have repeatedly stated that my perspective was from the Kingdom of God. This means that I was not going to limit these writings to how grace affects us in time but how grace operates in the eternal realm. There is a slight difficulty to this in that our language is reflective of time and not eternity, yet the text which we refer to is 2,000 years old and older. This is the paradox that we confront. Furthermore, since we are not familiar with the customs and practices of the times when the text was written, we try to attach present-day meanings to topics and occurrences that appear "un-natural" to us. So today I'm going to attack a present day mindset which limits our ability to access the nature of grace. I trust that when I'm through, the renewing of your mind will enable you to move into an elevated state of kingdom thinking. Prepare yourself for a journey.

Unmerited Favor

Ask any pastor or biblical teacher to define grace, and they will most commonly respond, "The unmerited favor of God." You have throughout these writings been probably harboring this definition in the back of your mind as an anchor to what you know. So why call it into question now? Is it possible that there may be more deception afoot then we've realized? The only way to determine this is to look at how the definition was arrived at and then determine if it is accurate enough to be the singular definition for grace. So let's take a look at how these two words are defined in order to bring them together in our text.

According to any good dictionary, you'll find the term "unmerited" defined as, "not earned or deserved." The word "favor" will have a more complex meaning depending on its use, such as the following:

noun	1. A gracious, friendly, or obliging act that is freely granted: *do someone a favor.*
	  • Friendly or favorable regard; approval or support: *won the favor of the monarch; looked with favor on the plan.*
	  • A state of being held in such regard: *a style currently in favor.*
	2. Unfair partiality; favoritism.
	  • A privilege or concession.
	  • Favors, sexual privileges, especially as granted by a woman.
	3. Something given as a token of love, affection, or remembrance.
	  • A small decorative gift given to each guest at a party.
	4. Advantage; benefit: *sailed under favor of cloudless skies.*
	5. Behalf; interest: *an error in our favor.*
	6. *Obsolete.* A communication, especially a letter.
	7. *Archaic.*
	  • Aspect or appearance.
	  • Countenance; face.

Verb	1. To perform a kindness or service for; oblige. 2. To treat or regard with friendship, approval, or support. 3. To be partial to; indulge a liking for: *favors bright colors.* 4. To be or tend to be in support of. 5. To make easier or more possible; facilitate: *Darkness favored their escape.* 6. To treat with care; be gentle with: *favored my wounded leg.*

I think from the information that we've gotten within these two words we can accurately describe **"unmerited favor"** as **an** unearned friendly act of favoritism given as a support or service. Is there anything in this definition which strikes you as odd? If not, then please carefully read it again because this is where we are going to go next.

Jesus, Our Pattern

> And the child grew, and waxed strong in spirit, filled with wisdom: and the **grace** of God was upon him. – Luke 2:40

> And the Word was made flesh, and dwelt among us, (and we beheld his glory, the glory as of the only begotten of the Father,) full of **grace** and truth. – John 1:14

In both of these passages, both Luke and John open their Gospel with a description of Jesus which includes how grace was operating through Him. If you, like me, have read these passages enough, you don't really stop to consider what these two writers are trying to say here. You just take the term "grace" at face value, or should I say at a value which doesn't require thinking. But let's consider this word "grace" now with the definition which we have from above and see if this sounds correct.

> And the child grew, and waxed strong in spirit, filled with wisdom: and the **unearned friendly act of favoritism given as a support or service** of God was upon him. – Luke 2:40 (revised)

> And the Word was made flesh, and dwelt among us, (and we beheld his glory, the glory as of the only begotten of the Father,) full of **the unearned friendly act of favoritism given as a support or service** and truth. – John 1:14 (revised)

Is it just me or does this somehow not "flow" the way it should? Maybe it's just the verse selection that doesn't work here; after all, grace does mean unmerited favor. Fair enough—let's try these two, also from Paul and John:

> And Jesus increased in wisdom and stature, and in **favor** with God and man. – Luke 2:52

> And of his fullness have all we received, and **grace** for **grace**. – John 1:16

Whoa! In the first verse, the word "favor" is the same word in the Greek we call "grace." So shouldn't that really read, "And Jesus increased in wisdom and stature, and in **unmerited favor** with God and man," while the second verse should read, "And of his fullness have all we received, and **unmerited favor** for **unmerited favor**." In the words of the famous poet Bugs Bunny, "What's up, doc?"

The Set Up

Okay, I admit that I set you up selecting these four verses. Notice I didn't have to go very far in either of these writer's Gospels to find the use of grace. Yet, I also want you to understand that the "pat" definition of grace will not work for every occurrence of the word "grace" which we come across in our reading. If I can do this with just four verses, what do you think a religious spirit can do with an entire doctrine? This is why I'm taking a defining approach with the topic of grace. I can safely say we've been set up, again. The question is, "How?"

The Cause

To understand this, we need to go back in time to when the Apostle Paul was in the city of Ephesus. Situated in the southwestern region of present day Turkey, Ephesus was the second largest city in both population and political importance in all of the Roman Empire. Historians believe John wrote his Gospel while residing in Ephesus, and this also established its position in the Book of Revelations, which he wrote some years later. Its prominence in the region had been established even before the reign of Alexander the Great. This was a thriving commercial metropolis which had been, and continued to be, at the crossroads of empires. Acts 19 describes Paul's entry into the city and his subsequent two year daily teaching ministry which he conducted in the city. I believe the church in this community was the apple of Paul's eye considering the manner in which he departed from them in Acts 20. Years later, while confined in a prison in Rome, Paul would write a letter to the church which some theologians call "the grandest glimpse into the heart of the Father." Contained within its opening passage is the longest sentence in the entire New Testament, comprised of eleven verses, which clearly establishes the plan and purpose of the Father before the foundations of the world. Yet, it is in the second chapter of this letter that our definition of "unmerited favor" is realized in the following verses:

*(6) And hath raised us up together, and made us sit together in heavenly places in Christ Jesus: (7) That in the ages to come he might shew the exceeding riches of his **grace** in his kindness toward us through Christ Jesus. (8) For by **grace** are ye saved through faith; and that not of yourselves: it is the gift of God: (9) **Not of works, lest any man should boast.** (10) For we are his workmanship, created in Christ Jesus unto good works, which God hath before ordained, that we should walk in them. – Ephesians 2:6-10*

Verse 8 establishes the fact that grace is a gift. This sentence covers the "favor" definition which we established above. The aspect of verse 9 is what defines the "unmerited" clause of the grace definition. If you, as many do, stop here, the definition of unmerited favor is correct and acceptable for almost every occurrence of the word grace. However, is it correct in context, both scripturally and historically? I would have to say...

Sitting next to what?

There is a deeper explanation to verse 9 which needs to be brought out here, and it involves verse 6. "...made us sit together in heavenly places in Christ Jesus." This establishes our position in God's Kingdom—a position that is shared with, and in, Christ. We are told in the book of Hebrews that Jesus sits at the right hand of the Father, which means that if He does, so do we. So for a moment, I want you to visualize you're sitting there, at the right hand of the Father. I want you to get a feel for how the seat feels on your skin; what it's like to hold onto the arms of the chair; to lean back into it. Take your time. There is no rush; after all, you belong there. Okay, now take your left hand and reach out to touch the chair beside you. Go ahead. Touch it. What did you just touch? That's right, the Father's throne—the Throne of Grace. Your Father just let you touch His throne. My question to you is this: Was that "unmerited favor" you just experienced? Before you answer that, consider this:

In a kingdom, the only people who are permitted to be on the same elevation as the king are family members. In the example above, you didn't have to reach up to the throne but across to the throne. Ephesians 1 tells us about how we became sons.

*(3) Blessed be the God and Father of our Lord Jesus Christ, who hath blessed us with every spiritual blessing in the heavenly places in Christ: (4) **even as he chose us in him before the foundation of the world,** that we should be holy and without blemish before him in love: (5) having **foreordained us unto adoption as sons through Jesus Christ unto himself,** according to the good pleasure of his will... – Ephesians 1:3-5*

Before time, before earth, you and I were chosen in Christ Jesus for adoption as sons. Now this is vitally important to understand, because the word for "son" which Paul uses here has special significance and relates solely to our discussion from the passage out of Ephesians 2. In the Greek vocabulary, there are two words for "son." There is one, which John uses in his writings, which describes a son that is born into the family, while the "son" Paul uses in his writings is for a son which is a legal heir to the family. The difference is that a legal heir has vested powers to act on behalf of the head of the family in every matter. This authority was often signified in public through an adoption ceremony. You can always be part of the family as a son, but you can only act as the father would act if society recognizes you're adopted. So how does this apply to our verses?

> BEING ADOPTED INTO THE HOUSEHOLD OF GOD MEANS THAT YOU HAVE THE LEGAL RIGHT TO ACT AS THE FATHER WOULD IN EVERY MATTER.

Paul is describing to the Ephesians how the Kingdom of God differs from the kingdoms of this world. In the first chapter of Ephesians, he clearly defines the pattern of the Kingdom of God. In the opening of the second chapter Paul shows the results achieved in the world system. By verse six, Paul has positioned us in heavenly places next to the throne, yet verse 9 explains the difference of how we arrived there according to a true operation of grace versus the manner in which all of Ephesus' society operated under.

In Roman societies of the day, it was quite common to "work" for positions of power, either through servitude or by buying favors from a benefactor. The ruling classes often adopted sons from other families in order to maintain an heir to their position. These arrangements were fully recognized within the social order of the day, and they were quite common in large cities like Rome and Ephesus, where the ability to rule depended on strong alliances across many family lines. What Paul is putting forth here in the second chapter is that position within God's Kingdom cannot be bought or sold, nor can you obtain it through any other manipulation of family structures. God had already predetermined what the protocol would be for entrance: It would be a gift of priceless value which for ages to come people would recognize.

If ye then, being evil, know how to give good gifts unto your children, how much more shall your Father which is in heaven give good things to them that ask him? – Matthew 7:11

Can "unmerited" be associated with "favor?"

So let's wrap up this matter of "unmerited favor." Is it warranted as a definition of grace? Let me ask you a few questions first. If you give your child a gift, is it unmerited? If you give your spouse a gift, is it unmerited? If your parents ever gave you a gift, was it unmerited? I believe the answer to each of these questions relies on the relationship that you have with the person. Personally speaking, I can say that every one of those questions can be answered with, "No, it was merited." My kids and spouse deserved every gift I gave them because of the love that I have for them, and I believe my parents felt the same way towards me. Yes, there may have been times where I tried to work for a gift or I had one of my children do the same thing to me. However, the result was never what was expected. I think we have allowed these two words to be joined together in an unholy alliance. They make about as much sense as the term "jumbo shrimp" or "long-haired bald man."

Our Father's plan and purpose has been established in eternity past, and He hasn't changed it. If Jesus found favor with Him and man, then we have the same nature available to us. But if we keep attaching "unmerited" to it, then it's no wonder we aren't doing the greater works which Jesus said that we should do. Even Paul says in Ephesians 2:10 that we've been pre-ordained to do those works, but if you believe that the grace which you operate in is unmerited, or not deserving, this is what you will get. This is leading me to...

Frustrating Grace

I do not frustrate the grace of God: for if righteousness comes by the law, then Christ is dead in vain. – Galatians 2:21

The book of Galatians is Paul's address to a body of believers who had been swayed by the religious spirit in certain Jewish practitioners. They were teaching the church in Galatia that they needed to begin to perform the rituals of the Law as a means to practicing their faith in God and the works of Jesus. In this book, Paul lays out a very concise argument for faith in the work of Christ, yet in doing so, he draws attention to this concept of frustrating grace. This is the foremost problem that the believer has to confront in their life as they move into the kingdom mentality. Religious spirits utilize this as a tool to control a believer, which I'll demonstrate in a moment.

What is so frustrating?

We all know what frustration is and have at one time or another been hampered by it, so I don't need to define it for you. I decided to look at how the various translators used this word in this passage. Terms such as make void, set aside, repudiate, and nullify are all being used to describe "frustrate." Obviously with terms such as these, it might be better to understand what could possibly be behind this "frustration."Let me explain it with a very simple and oh-so-common experience.

Have you ever presented a gift to someone who you cared about, a gift which you spent either a significant amount of time finding or money acquiring, only to hear this from them: "Oh! You shouldn't have. I can't take this." In this exchange, how often have you responded, "Yes, I got it for you. Please take it," only to hear, "No, I can't. It's too much." In someone's life, the process of this one exchange may have become very protracted and ended in a manner which was the complete opposite to what was intended. Guess what? This entire scenario is known as *frustrating grace*. But how is that possible?

> *Every good* gift and *every perfect* gift is from above, and *cometh down from the Father* of lights, with whom is no variableness, neither shadow of turning. – James 1:17

When someone uses the term "every," what is left out? Not one thing, correct? So James tells us that a gift which is good and perfect in its nature (why wouldn't any gift have these characteristics?) is all-inclusive in its scope too, and these types of gifts come from the Father. "But what does this have to do with the necklace that I tried to give to my daughter-in-law or the new car that I tried to give to my son and his wife? I was the one giving it to them." If you are that naïve, please suspend your belief for a moment. A growth spurt is about to happen. Understand that God uses us to promote the kingdom in the lives of those around us, and one of the methods which He employs is the giving of gifts. (This is what grace is about after all! The next chapter will expand on this further.)

The Culprit

But what is behind these actions, either by others or by our self towards others? Those who are endowed with a religious spirit will say that their humility keeps them from being overcome by the trappings of this world. I have to say this is very honorable—and a whole lot of lawn fertilizer from farm animals too! (You know what I mean.) The true name for this false sense of humility is called "pride." Before you get all puckered up here, you better understand why I make this claim. When we make the claim that we can't take a gift for "X" reason, we have displayed our "choke point," or self-imposed limitation on what the Kingdom of God is able to place in our lives. Grace's nature is to give and do it abundantly, but God will not give beyond what you're

> SINCE EVERY GOOD AND PERFECT GIFT COMES FROM THE FATHER, ANY TIME THAT YOU ARE UNABLE TO ACCEPT A GIFT FROM ANYONE THIS REVEALS A CHOKE POINT FOR RECEIVING FURTHER FROM THE FATHER.

capable of receiving. God already gave the greatest gift of all through His son Jesus, and every gift is simply an extension leading us back to that gift. Remember it is the goodness of God which leads all men to repentance.

When we choke on a gift, we are saying in essence, "No, I can't take this. Jesus didn't give enough for me; I'm the only one who can give what's required." I realize this statement doesn't sound pretty (or smell pretty for that matter!), but pride at its inner-most core acts this way. "Well, I never..." Please stop for a moment and consider this: Have you ever wondered why Jesus said that we should approach the kingdom like little children? Have you ever seen a little child **turn down a gift**? A child knows nothing of pride until they meet an adult who wants to control their actions.

Religious spirits act the same way and want to control your actions by helping the homeless, childless, orphaned, pregnant, drug addicts and convicts of the world as a means of showing your worthiness, since obviously your tithes and offerings are not moving God to work on your behalf. Even the mere tokens (gifts) which are placed before you are there to lure you into an unholy acceptance for the things of this world, which we all know will perish in the end anyway, keeping you from... Do I need to go on here?

The Rule of the Kingdom of Grace

Gifts, in all of their variety of forms, come from the Father. They have been preordained to aid you in the works that have been prepared for you long before the foundations of this world were even laid. These gifts point you to the goodness of your Father, and no matter how it is delivered to you, its sole purpose is to cause you to offer abundant thanks to the Father for His great love for you. When any gift is presented to you, the rule of the Kingdom of Grace is simple: Always take the gift. In doing so, you keep the abounding environment of grace functioning in your life.

Remember: Always take the gift.

1.5 Good Gifts

At this point, there are a couple of passages I want to bring to your attention regarding "goodness."

*Or do you despise **the riches of His goodness**, forbearance, and longsuffering, not knowing that **the goodness of God** leads you to **repentance**? – Romans 2:4*

God's goodness leads us to repentance. I'm not going to get all religious here, but do you understand what it means to "repent?" Religion has built up an edifice around the term which keeps people from its simple truth and, unfortunately, keeps a number of people out of the kingdom. Traditionally the term means to show sorrow for acts committed that may have wounded or injured another. In relation to God it means sorrow for a sin which violates His holy law. There is something more in the word that should be revealed. The suffix "re" has the meaning of returning back to the original condition or state of being. The word "pent" has a number of meanings in its usage—one being the high place as in the term "penthouse." Another is the Greek term which represents the numeric value of five, a number Bible scholars all agree represents "grace." So repenting means more than acting in a sorrowful state about a sin; it holds in it the ability to return us back to our original high position of grace. Yet notice in this verse only one thing leads us to this act of repenting: The goodness of God.

Now I want you to see something about this from the life of Moses. In Exodus 33, God has brought the children of Israel out of Egypt, and Moses has ascended up Mount Sinai for the second time. In this chapter, Moses encounters something very unique about the nature of God as he confirms that God will be with them as they proceed into the Promised Land.

> *(12) Then Moses said to the LORD, "See, You say to me, 'Bring up this people.' But You have not let me know whom You will send with me. Yet You have said, 'I know you by name, and you have also found **grace** in My sight. (13) Now therefore, I pray, if I have found **grace** in Your sight, **show me now Your way, that I may know You** and that I may find **grace** in Your sight. And consider that this nation is Your people.(14) And He said, "My Presence will go with you, and I will give you rest.(15) Then he said to Him, "If Your Presence does not go with us, do not bring us up from here. (16) For how then will it be known that Your people and I have found **grace** in Your sight, except You go with us? So we shall be separate, Your people and I, from all the people who are upon the face of the earth.(17) So the LORD said to Moses, "I will also do this thing that you have spoken; for you have found **grace** in My sight, and I know you by name.(18) And he said, **"Please, show me Your glory.(19)** Then He said, "**<u>I will make all My goodness pass before you</u>**, and I will proclaim the name of the LORD before you. I will be **gracious** to whom I will be **gracious**, and I will have compassion on whom I will have compassion.(20) But He said, "You cannot see My face; for no man shall see Me, and live." – Exodus 33:12-20*

I have stated before that the meaning of the Hebrew term for grace is different than the Greek term for grace. It cannot be ignored, but it needs to be incorporated into the full meaning of grace (which space does not permit me to develop here). In this passage, we see Moses found grace in the sight of God, and he asks that God would show him the ways of God so Moses would know

God. What occurs next is a fulfillment of Moses' request. Moses asks to see the glory of God. He wants to see all of what defines the Kingdom of God. Recall that Moses, when he was in Egypt as a member of Pharaoh's household, was in the heart of the display of man's kingdom glory. His request here in verse 18 was a natural response to see the abundance of a kingdom in order to assure the greatness of a king.

Don't assume for a moment here that Moses is judging the Kingdom of God. When kings come in union with one another it is common for each to display the abundance which each realm contains, because out of this abundance, gifts will be presented one to another as a display of the "grace" of the kingdom. Moses' request here is really an application to understand the protocol of the Kingdom of God in order that he may be able to properly represent the children of Israel in the Kingdom of God. Yet notice what God's response to Moses is: "I will make all My goodness pass before you." This statement defines the ways of God. His goodness, not His glory, is how the kingdom is recognized and operates. It is not defined by all of its wealth of material items but by the nature of the King Himself.

What is important here is God clearly demonstrates that a kingdom display of any material objects does not make any reference to how those objects were obtained. Things can be given, bought, or stolen, yet once obtained, no one truly knows how they arrived, let alone how they are retained. If we merely look upon things and say this is truly a king of many resources, we fail to know the true nature of the king and, ultimately, the kingdom itself. By clearly distinguishing that His kingdom comes out of His goodness, God has declared that whatever "things" we see of Him, they all come from His nature of goodness. So as the book of James tells us, "Every good and perfect gift comes from the Father." This is not an indication of His wealth, but it's out of His goodness towards us—a goodness which leads us back to the high place of grace.

Grace to Give

So now you're ready to start acting like your Father, the King. This means you're going to have to begin to understand the nature of giving from the kingdom perspective. This concept of giving is best viewed in the act of exchanging a gift. The premier verse which explains the grace-gift exchange is John 3:16:

> For God **so loved** the world, that **he gave** his only begotten Son, that whosoever believeth in him should not perish, but **have everlasting life.**

Yes, this verse is truly an expression of the nature of the Kingdom of Grace. Yet since we've not understood the nature of grace, we miss the awesome treasures that reside in this one verse. We have been using it as a salvation verse to implore the lost that God truly loves them and has forgiven them. You just read in the nature of abounding grace there is an honor which grace places upon anything associated with life. We see here that everlasting life is the reciprocal grace-gift given in believing in God's Son.

I want to take a moment to look further into this aspect of reciprocal giving and bring attention to a component of the ancient Greek thought which we have long overlooked. Tell me if this sounds familiar. You've been invited to a party given by a distant relative who you've never been really close to. A couple of hours prior to the party, you're told an aunt of yours will be attending the same party. This aunt has always been the type to pour out gifts to everyone no matter what the occasion, and you've been the proud recipient of a number of her gifts over the years. While it had never been your intention to bring a gift, now you feel obligated to bring a gift to "offset" the gift which you know she will have for you. The circumstances may be different, but the feeling of "offsetting" is what you always experience. Welcome to the nature of reciprocal giving.

A Higher Level of Giving

Where I'm now about to take you is into the heavenly realm of how the Kingdom of God views this matter. We have been looking at most of this reciprocal giving from the perspective of mankind's social interactions, yet as we ascend into the heavenly places where we are seated at the right hand of the throne of grace with Jesus, we are going to begin to see an entirely different nature to the purpose of giving.

> THE ABILITY TO GIVE A GIFT TO SOMEONE IN ADVANCE OF WHEN THEY WILL NEED IT IS A DISPLAY OF GRACE IN ACTION. IN THE KINGDOM, THIS IS KNOWN AS FORGIVENESS.

The first thing which you will notice seated in the heavenly realm is that time truly is a line with a start and end—both of which you can see in the same moment. This is different from when you're in time, since all you can see is what is directly in front of you (future) or what is directly behind you (history) but never both at once. The distance which you are able to see in time is dictated by the significant events which you've established in either direction. In history, it is a series of significant emotional events you are able to recall at will, while in the future, it is a pre-determined goal which you are striving for.

From an eternal, kingdom perspective there is always the ability to see beyond the perspective of anybody's sight in time, history or future. This enables a facet of the nature of grace which I call "forward giving," or the ability to give a gift in advance of when the gift is truly needed. Let me explain with an example.

When I was in my early twenties, one year for Christmas, my grandfather gave me a gift which I felt was rather out of left field. He had gone to great lengths to assemble a package of items that would help in the event my car ever broke down. There was a hazard flashlight, flares, emergency signs, and a whole assortment of devices which could be used to help in the event of a flat tire or mechanical emergency while on the road. The reason I felt that it was out of left field was because I didn't own a car at the time; I rode a bicycle. I recall at the time it being difficult to appreciate the benefit of such a gift, yet I reluctantly accepted it and immediately put it in a box which subsequently sat in storage for a number of years.

After I was married, I retrieved the box from storage and placed the contents in the trunk of my car, which I now owned. About a month later, I was driving down the road, and suddenly, my tire blew out. When I got to the side of the road, I went to the trunk of my car and pulled out all of the equipment which my grandfather had given to me so many years past. I was greatly appreciative of every item in that gift on the day when I needed it.

The Kingdom of God has the same benefits set aside for each of us. The nature of forward giving in the kingdom comes from the throne of grace which sits over the line of time and is able to see in your life when you will need the benefit that can only come from a heavenly gift. This ability to give a gift in a forward nature is expected of every person who is seated in heavenly places. You'll find mention of it in a number of scriptures, yet for now, the following one will be our highlight:

> *Bearing with one another, and **forgiving** one another, if anyone has a complaint against another; even as Christ **forgave** you, so you also must do. But above all these things put on **love**, which is the bond of perfection. – Colossians 3:13-14*

Forward giving, or "forgiving" as you'll find it in the Bible, is a function of grace. Both the word "forgiving" and "forgave" are grace words representing another facet of the nature of grace which has been lost. Notice in this passage that as we act in a grace-manner we are representing the works of Christ from His throne of grace. Our ability to "forward-give" to one another enables the recipient of the gift to overcome a difficulty in a future place, where what they received from us has perfected them in love to handle the moment with the grace of the kingdom. The reciprocal nature of grace will also insure you of a similar result in your future.

This is the high ground of grace which many are unaware of, since forgiveness has such an emotional stronghold attached to it. Realize that the act of forgiveness is actually a gift used to overcome an advanced obstacle in the life of another. This places a new level of authority upon our actions which we've never possibly walked in. Yes, there may be pain attached to the matter between you and another, but you hold in your hand the opportunity to see to it that they succeed in a future mission which fulfills their destiny. Failure to forgive only delays success for them as well as for you.

Remember this: God, because of His great love for us, joyously gave a reciprocal-grace gift through His Son, Jesus, far in advance of when we would need it so that we could victoriously claim the overwhelming life which comes to us through His love for us.

1.6 Man's Purpose in Grace

Now that you better understand the nature of "good," I want you to recall the creation event described in Genesis 1 and the seven references to the term "good." You should be able to recognize that each event demonstrated not only the capabilities of God merely to create, but that they represented His nature in why and how He created. In every occurrence, when you read "It was good," you are reliving exactly what Moses experienced on the Mount as the goodness of God passed before him. Understanding goodness also provides you with the ability to recognize when it is lacking. Did you know the creation event provides an example of this?

> *(4) This is the history of the heavens and the earth when they were created, in the day that the LORD God made the earth and the heavens,(5) before any plant of the field was in the earth and before any herb of the field had grown. For the LORD God had not caused it to rain on the earth, and there was no man to till the ground;(6) but a mist went up from the earth and watered the whole face of the ground.(7) And the LORD God formed man of the dust of the ground, and breathed into his nostrils the breath of life; and man became a living being.(8) The LORD God planted a garden eastward in Eden, and there He put the man whom He had formed. – Genesis 2:4-8*

Chapter 1 of Genesis describes the creation events from day one to six, culminating with the proclamation that all which God had created was "very good." The second chapter starts with God setting apart and blessing the seventh day as a day of rest for man.

We pick up in verse 4 an expansion of the narrative of the sixth day, operating fully in the nature of grace, to see how things progressed towards the ultimate proclamation. Verse 5 tells us the plants were waiting for the creation of man in order for them to begin to grow, since the ground hadn't been tilled yet, even though it was being watered from the mist which was coming up out of the earth. In the seventh verse, we discover that God formed man from the dust of the earth and breathed into his nostrils the breath of life.

The term "formed" in verse 7 describes a process similar to the manipulations which a potter performs when drawing out the desired form of a piece of clay through the use of pressure. Considering that the man was created from the dust of the earth, this is an appropriate description of how God formed man. This is also the only indication in creation that God used His hands to create an object. All other elements appear to be created from God's word or command. This distinction can't be stressed enough since God declared that man was to be like Him in image and likeness. All other items were dictated as to their purpose and existence, while man's formation indicates the free will purpose which marks man's existence.

(15) Then the LORD God took the man and put him in the garden of Eden to tend and keep it.(16) And the LORD God commanded the man, saying, "Of every tree of the garden you may freely eat; (17) but of the tree of the knowledge of good and evil you shall not eat, for in the day that you eat of it you shall surely die." (18) And the LORD God said, "It is not good that man should be alone; I will make him a helper comparable to him." (19) Out of the ground the LORD God formed every beast of the field and every bird of the air, and brought them to Adam to see what he would call them. And whatever Adam called each living creature, that was its name. (20) So Adam gave names to all

cattle, to the birds of the air, and to every beast of the field. But for Adam there was not found a helper comparable to him. – Genesis 2:15-20

We see in verse 8 after man became a living being, God placed him in a garden east of where he was formed. As ideal as the Garden of Eden is, man was not created in it; he shares none of the properties of that environment. In verse 15, we see that the man is contracted to be there for God's purpose of tending and keeping it. If the man had been originally created in the garden, he would have immediate dominion over the area, and God would not be able to displace him from his "domain" except through battle. By placing the man in the garden, God is indicating that the tending and keeping of the garden placed an expectation towards a moment of completion or subjection for dominion to be conferred. Any failure in achieving this end would result in the delay of dominion. Every kingdom must be fought for to be awarded and retained. This is what Jesus meant when He said that the Kingdom of God suffers violence, and the violent take it by force.

So what does it mean that man was placed in the garden to "tend and keep it?" Each of these words has separate and very distinct meanings as to the purpose which the man was to fulfill. The Hebraic meaning of the word recorded as "tend" carries the meaning of "to till the ground as a husbandman or laborer." Much of society has lost its understanding of tilling as we have moved away from an agricultural social order towards a specialized, industrial social order. We miss the nature of tilling—to turn over and expose hidden matter; of the preparation of the soil to receive the seed; of the focus of keeping weeds from overtaking the crop; and of feeding the soil the nutrients required to promote the growth of the seed. This same word also is used to describe a servant and worshipper. So we see here that man's job to till the garden involved uncovering hidden things, preparing a place for seed to be implanted and nourished. These all acted as a service of worship towards God.

The Hebrew word for "keep" in this passage means to be a watchman or a guard which watches with a very narrow, intentional gaze. It implies that the person is responsible for overseeing the life of the garden by restraining any invading force. So we see that there were two functions that man was to perform while employed in the garden: worshipful service to the seed of God's creative word and protector of the environment which the seed was to produce its fruit in. In verses 16 and 17, we see the contract restriction to man's employment with God in the garden. It clearly defines that all of the work being performed in the garden had a limit upon man's ability to enjoy all the rewards from those efforts.

God's Gift to Man

But as great as the garden is, please understand this was not a gift to man. It was man's work, duty or service. Today, we often make the mistake of thanking God for the gift of our work. I'm not saying that we shouldn't thank God for work, but our employment, whatever it may be, is not a gift from the grace realm. Yes, I realize some of you may disagree with me about this, but consider this: Proverbs 10:22 tells us the blessing of the Lord, while making you rich, does not add sorrow to it. A job, while it can make you rich, also will add sorrow. If every good and perfect gift comes from the Father, contained in the gift is the blessing of the Father. This blessing activates the abundant nature of grace in the gift, making it a life-giving property to all who come in contact with it. If you claim that God blessed you with a job as a gift of His grace, I simply have to ask you, is this gift giving life to all who come in contact with it, and will this principle continue to operate if you're not involved in it? Employment is our worship to God, where we demonstrate the nature of His kingdom to those who do not know Him.

So returning to our man in the garden, verse 18 must stand out in this study, as well as any other study of God's handiwork. In this verse, we hear God declare that something isn't good, meaning it lacks the pleasure associated with the Kingdom of Grace. Notice God is declaring this about man, not about God's Kingdom. Man was created to be in the likeness and image of God, and yet God declares that man being alone is not good or doesn't align with the principle of kingdom grace. Throughout the entire creation event, we have seen "goodness" was God's final declaration, yet man's existence is deemed "not good" if he is alone. Another way of saying this is the pleasure of grace is not complete in the life of man when there is no one to give to.

God's decree of "not good" also contains within it the answer whih will correct the matter and bring it to completion. God will make a helper comparable to the man. But look what follows: Adam names the animals—no helper, just names the animals. What gives here? This is one of the examples of the ways of God.

As I stated a moment ago, God declared it was not good for man to be alone. Man did not make this observation, God did. Man didn't yet know that there was something amiss. The Hebrew teachers say that the reason God had Adam name the animals first was so that he could see for himself that there was something different between the pairings of the animals with the commission which God had placed upon them to be fruitful and multiply and himself with the same commission. Only after he had completed this task could he fully recognize and understand that he did not have a partner to fulfill his commission. We often are called to perform a task for God's kingdom not recognizing what we discover in our performance is the missing element in us fulfilling our commission.

> (21) And the LORD God caused a deep sleep to fall on Adam, and he slept; and He took one of his ribs, and closed up the flesh in its place.(22) Then the rib which the LORD God had taken from man **He made into a woman, and He brought her to the man.** (23) And Adam said: "This is now bone of my bones And flesh of my flesh; She shall be called Woman, Because she was taken out of Man." — Genesis 2:21-23

In the creation event, we see the workings of abounding grace in that everything which is made comes from the environment where it resides and abounds: stars made from the elements of space; birds from the elements of the sky; fish from the elements of the water; and beasts from the elements of the earth. Man too is made from the earth, yet different from the animals, since God formed him and breathed life into his body. His body abounds upon the earth, while his spirit abounds in the eternal realm. Now we see the last creation act of God was making a woman out of an element of man. This element, the rib, tells us that the woman is to abound at the side of man, not at his foot, his head, or his backside.

An important aspect of grace which many overlook has to do with honor. This honor is evident in the kingdom by the presence of the throne of grace. As grace operated in the creation event, the highest honor is given to each object which reflects the fullness of the elements it came from. Man received the highest honor of being the fullness of not only the dust of the earth but the image of God also. In this same manner, the woman receives the highest honor being made from man. This is not an honor of authority over man but as a crown upon man.

In verse 22, we find something unique about this creative act. Here we find God "made" the woman. This word is entirely different from the word which described how God made man. This word conveys the picture of God going away to a place to design and fashion the woman with serious intent. Upon the completion of this creative act, we are told God "brought" her to the man. The word "brought" portrays the act of giving or setting down. *In this verse, we witness the goodness and grace of the King giving a "crown" as a "gift" to the man.* Said another way, the woman is the first grace-gift to man. Yes, despite what you may feel or have heard in the past, <u>a woman is a gift from God to man, purposely designed and fashioned to work alongside and provide honor to man.</u>

I feel it is best to stop here for a moment. That last statement needs to be fully ingested before you go forward, since what occurs next is entirely dependent upon your understanding this truth.

1.7 Review

At this junction, we need to review some of what has been said. You've probably never read or even considered some of the things which have crossed your mind in these previous pages. This is why I'm stopping for a moment. It's possible that you need to reconsider whether what you thought about grace can hold up to what has been shown here or not. I say this because your journey hasn't even begun to ascend to the height that God has intended you to travel. Yet these points are essential principles in recognizing and accessing the nature of grace along your path.

So this is a time to stop and catch your breath and reflect on what has just come into your field of vision. Use the following statements and questions as a means of collecting your thoughts.

1. Before I began this book, I believed that grace was:

   _____

   _____

   _____

   _____

2. How did knowing when grace began affect your understanding of it?

   _____

   _____

   _____

   _____

3. How does knowing what the Greeks understood about *charis* change the way which you now interpret grace when you read your Bible?

_____

_____

_____

_____

_____

4. What aspect of the nature of reciprocal giving or even forward giving do you believe has been neglected in your life?

_____

_____

_____

_____

5. I believe that going boldly before the throne of grace means:

_____

_____

_____

_____

6. How does knowing the role of grace in the creation events affect your perspective of the role of the man and the woman?

_____

_____

_____

_____

7. Describe how your past view of God's goodness has been impacted by understanding its connection now with grace.

_____

_____

_____

_____

_____

8. I now understand that grace is:

_____

_____

_____

_____

This completes our primary study of grace, which will give you the foundational understanding required to move into the remaining parts of this book. If you wish to get even a more thorough grasp of this topic, consider going to **www.mygrace2u.com** for more material and resources.

Part 2
Shame

"SEE! THOSE FIENDISH LINEAMENTS GRAVEN ON THE DARKNESS, THE WRITHED LIP OF SCORN, THE MOCKERY OF THAT LIVING EYE, THE POINTED FINGER, TOUCHING THE SORE PLACE IN YOUR HEART! DO YOU REMEMBER ANY ACT OF ENORMOUS FOLLY, AT WHICH YOU WOULD BLUSH, EVEN IN THE REMOTEST CAVERN OF THE EARTH? THEN RECOGNIZE YOUR SHAME."

NATHANIEL HAWTHORNE

2.1 The Start of Shame

Grace Unplugged

A number of years ago, the music industry became fascinated with the aspect of "unplugged" performances. It became a new medium of entertainment to well-established musicians to switch from the "electrical" format to an acoustical format. The natural, simplistic format which acoustic sound provided to the standard pieces these artists had previously performed lent a whole new level of respect to the artistic quality of many of the performers. In a similar vein, we are going to look at what happened when grace went acoustical and the sight and sound which it produced.

Grace Plugged In

The first two chapters of Genesis depict the fullest manifestation of grace in operation which we have record of prior to Jesus. In these chapters, we catch a glimpse of what the Father's original intent was, and still is, for man and how we are to operate through the grace which comes from the kingdom.

At the end of six days of grace's creative expression, man and woman stood as its apex. Their first day functioning in the grace which God had deposited in the earth was to be spent in the rest of the Father. Their purpose upon this earth began in a rest ordained by the Father. In that day of rest, they experienced the fullness of the Creator in ways which we can only imagine as they explored the realm that had been established for them. Fully man, the image and likeness of the living God, eternal, and empowered with the grace and honor which befits a royal line, Adam and the woman stand to many as the figurehead of what mankind lost rather than what we are supposed to be like prior to the fall.

What happened to the power?

The third chapter of Genesis provided us with the events which caused what everyone refers to as "the fall of man." I have come to recognize these events are what caused the "disconnect" from the grace of the Kingdom of God, which affected his ability to access the Kingdom of God.

When I began this whole study of grace, I was focused entirely upon what have we missed in the definition of grace and how it is supposed to function in our lives beyond the standard "saved by grace" mentality. Over the weeks, months, and now years, I have found there is also a facet that needs to be explored in order to fully explain what is missing. This facet is what the effect of the loss of grace was. Sure, we have all some understanding of it, but according to its truest meaning, we have no clue what it means to be out of grace or even recognize when we are. In other words, if you know what God knows about being disconnected from grace, or disgrace, then you'll be able to know what the enemy will use to keep you out of the Kingdom of God.

The First Fall from Grace

This study would not be complete if I didn't mention the enemy of God. satan, or lucifer, was an anointed cherub created by God

---

and responsible for leading the angelic realm in the worship of God. Ezekiel 28:12-16 and Isaiah 14:12-14 tell of what led to his fall from the kingdom. These verses do not provide us with a timeframe of when the fall occurred in relation to the creation of man. But what they do provide is a description of what he looked like before the fall and how his pride for the position which he held led to his expulsion. I want to draw your attention to a part of the description from Ezekiel.

> *(13) Thou hast been in Eden the garden of God; every precious stone was thy covering, the sardius, topaz, and the diamond, the beryl, the onyx, and the jasper, the sapphire, the emerald, and the carbuncle, and gold: the workmanship of thy tabrets and of thy pipes was prepared in thee in the day that thou was created.(14) Thou art the anointed cherub that covers; and I have set thee so: thou was upon the holy mountain of God; thou hast walked up and down in the midst of the stones of fire. – Ezekiel 28:13-14*

In this passage is a reference to him being in the Garden of Eden. Also, I want you to see the description of the covering which clothed him in his position as the anointed cherub. Lastly, notice in verse 14, he was a cherub that "covers." This was his purpose, to cover God, or protect and defend the King of Grace. Whenever God moved, this anointed cherub would proceed before Him with the angelic host of worshippers in a posture of protection. The passage from Isaiah informs us that his pride to be exalted above God was the factor which expelled him from his vaulted position. This backdrop of the enemy gives us a look at the tactics he will employ in the garden to wrestle the earth from out of the hands of man.

Paradise Lost

Now the serpent was more cunning than any beast of the field which the LORD God had made. And he said to the woman, "Has God indeed said, 'You shall not eat of every tree of the garden'?"
— Genesis 3:1

This first verse in chapter three is very distinct in a number of ways. We see here that the enemy came as a serpent in the Garden, but his appearance was radically different from what was recorded in Ezekiel. Obviously, a snake is a radical departure from a cherub, but what is significant is the term "cunning" used in this passage. While it does mean "crafty and cunning," its primary meaning in Hebrew is "to be or make bare." In this description, we see that the enemy had lost all of his covering and was bare before the woman.

Another distinction to be made here is that the snake speaks. This is not something many believe could have happened, simply because it doesn't happen today. I want you to understand this one thing: The Kingdom of God is not like anything we've ever experienced: Donkeys talking, ax heads floating, and virgins giving birth to kings are just a few of the "normal" occurrences we discount as "unbelievable"—a matter which will be addressed in a moment.

> THE KINGDOM OF GOD IS NOT LIKE ANYTHING THAT YOU'VE EVER EXPERIENCED: DONKEYS TALKING, AX HEADS FLOATING, AND VIRGINS GIVING BIRTH TO KINGS ARE JUST A FEW OF ITS "NORMAL" OCCURRENCES.

Consider this: The person who the enemy speaks to in this drama is the crown jewel of God's creation—a similar position which he once occupied in the kingdom. The woman, as I have stated previously, held the highest honorable position in the creation—a position which if compromised would mean the subjection of all things below it. Tarnish the crown, and it affects the entire kingdom. Many miss this very fine point by thinking that the enemy's attack was on the "weaker" vessel. It had nothing to do with strength but everything to do with a position lost and wanting to be regained. The enemy is only concerned with one thing: being worshipped. Nothing else matters to him. He will use whatever means necessary to make this occur.

So we now have in place an understanding of the condition of the enemy and what he intends to accomplish in this dialogue. He understood that there was no authority for him to do anything on the earth since God had placed it in the hands of man. He had to get the man to willfully turn over his realm if he was going to have any power. This could only be done by disconnecting the link which man had with the eternal kingdom—a disconnect which had been clearly specified by God himself in commissioning man's work in the garden: "...for in the day that you eat of it (tree of the knowledge of good and evil), you shall surely die."

> (2) And the woman said to the serpent, "We may eat the fruit of the trees of the garden; (3) but of the fruit of the tree which is in the midst of the garden, God has said, 'You shall not eat it, **nor shall you touch it**, lest you die.' " (4) Then the serpent said to the woman, "You will not surely die. (5) For God knows that in the day you eat of it **your eyes will be opened**, and you will be like God, knowing good and evil. – Genesis 3:2-5

If you've been around any teaching of these events in the past, there is always mention of what the woman added to the condition

God set before man about the fruit of the tree. The Hebrew scholars state that the additional information the woman provided is due to the fact that the enemy had pushed the woman next to the tree, and by forcing her to touch it, he was able to demonstrate that death wouldn't occur, making the woman doubt if what God had said was true.

Belief to Doubt: A Road Most Traveled

The number one tool which the enemy uses against everyone on the face of this earth is the tool of doubt. He knows that if the seed of doubt can be planted, it will grow on its own, fed entirely on circumstances. I mentioned a moment ago about the unique characteristics of the Kingdom of God, and you were given a number of instances from the operations of the kingdom where you either believe or doubt. There is no middle ground—either yes or no. The enemy operates more in the "middle ground" than at either of the other two poles. He knows God's truth, and if you align with it, you are aligning with God, which is something he hates. He knows he cannot get you to shift from knowing a truth to denying it in one move. So he strategically uses doubt to subtly move you from belief to unbelief.

> THE NUMBER ONE TOOL THAT THE ENEMY USES AGAINST EVERYONE ON THE FACE OF THIS EARTH IS THE TOOL OF DOUBT.

Let me give you an example: The Word of God states we are healed by the stripes that Jesus bore on his back. This is a kingdom truth. This is how God sees you today, right now. If you have never been sick a day in your life, you align with this truth. But most of us have at one time or another been sick. These circumstances never negate the truth of the kingdom, yet the enemy uses them to build a case of doubt about the truth in God's Word. Every sickness, disease or ailment acts as another seed of doubt. The enemy uses this principle for every truth and promise God has given to us. He knows that time is on his side simply because it reinforces the doubt when things don't happen when we expect them to happen.

In these few verses, we see this very principle in action. The serpent has planted the thought which runs contrary to the truth that God has spoken. This is accomplished in verse one with the statement, "Has God indeed said..." Thus begins the cycle of having to prove the truth.

Truth doesn't need to be proven for it to be truth, but our insecurities in truly knowing and living a truth causes us to over-extend ourselves and try to prove a truth we haven't fully assimilated. This is what is occurring in verses 2 and 3 as the woman conveys what she knows about the restrictions which have been placed upon the trees in the garden.

For doubt to function, it has to create a thought in you which is different from the one thought that you have been fixated on. The thought has to be equal to or greater in value to what you presently obtain from your original thought. The enemy knows that thoughts of equal value are the hardest to establish a basis of doubt with. So the ploy which is often used is to accentuate a difference—even if it has no bearing upon the matter at hand—and then place the difference between the similarities and establish a greater reward available in the second thought due to its difference. This takes place in verses 4 and 5.

In these verses, can you spot the similarities and the one difference? The similarity is that Adam and the woman are made in the likeness and image of God, so they are eternal beings incapable of dying also. The difference is in the eyes. This is what the enemy will use to thwart any belief about the kingdom you possess. You might ask, "But how is this possible?" Give me a brief moment, and I'll show you.

The 11th chapter of the book of Hebrews is known at the "Hall of Faith." Recorded in this chapter are all the great and mighty people of the Bible who had faith, or belief, in God. A foundational principle in the chapter is that it is impossible to please God without faith (belief). In 2 Corinthians chapter 5, Paul tells us, "we live by faith and not by sight." Put another way, we live by what we believe in, not by what our eyes see around us. Link this to the prior verse I mentioned, and it is expanded like this: God is happy with us when we live by what we believe in rather than what our eyes see about us.

What the enemy did was cause the woman to doubt what she knew, or believed, about God's words. Knowing her belief is what was pleasing to God, the enemy called into question the woman's ability to see correctly, since any reliance on her natural sight to bolster her belief would work to his advantage of strengthening her doubt. In order for her to rely more on her sight than her belief, he created a deficiency in her god-like character and linked it to the use of her eyes.

The eyes have it.

*And when the woman **saw** that the tree was good for food, and that it was **pleasant** to the **eyes**, and a tree to be **desired** to make one wise, she took of the fruit thereof, and did eat, and* **gave also unto her husband with her; and he did eat.**
– Genesis 3:6

How many times have you seen something and said to yourself, "I've got to have that," only to regret it later? This is the working of the enemy on your soul. The woman, the crown of God's creation, caught between belief and doubt, battled an attack on her soul.

The word "pleasant" and "desired" are two separate Hebrew words which both have the meaning of lusting, or coveting for, the very actions that expelled the enemy from the Kingdom of Heaven. Coveting any item is a direct attack on grace because its intent is not based on giving but on hoarding. Hoarding often operates when there is a perceived sense of lack or where an item of value is limited. In this verse, we see both of these in operation: A single tree produces a fruit reported to increase wisdom.

Our greatest attacks from the enemy are those which pit our soul against the kingdom simply by allowing our eyes to create a picture contrary to the kingdom and then letting our thoughts associate an intense desire to posses it.

What did Adam see?

In the latter portion of this verse, we witness the progression of the woman's actions: Seeing and coveting the fruit, she took and ate it and then gave it to her husband and he ate it. Many people just pass over this aspect of the narrative without considering what

Grace for Shame

truly was happening. However, if you want to understand how grace operates, even at this junction, there are few things which you had better recognize, and they surround the actions of Adam.

Recall God told Adam that in the day that he eats the fruit from the tree of knowledge of good and evil, he will surely die (Genesis 2:17). We know even though he ate it, he didn't "die" that day but 930 years later. Some would take this and say that God is a liar, but while Adam didn't die in body on that day, he did die in spirit. It was their spirits which linked the man and woman to the kingdom of grace. But it was the woman that ate the fruit first. In the moment before Adam ate, what did he see or witness in his wife? Obviously, she did not die in body at that moment either, but something happened which he hadn't expected.

> IF YOU WANT TO UNDERSTAND THE ACTIONS OF ADAM IN THE GARDEN, THEN YOU NEED TO UNDERSTAND THE ACTIONS OF JESUS IN THE GARDEN OF GETHSEMANE. THE LAST ADAM WILL CORRECT THE RESULTS FROM THE FIRST ADAM.

Many Bible scholars believe that Adam and the woman were clothed in the same glory which clouds God himself. A vibrant, living light which also was characteristic of the glory that Moses experienced on Mount Sinai and subsequently wore upon him when he came down to the children of Israel. Following this thought, consider that when the woman ate of the fruit, this glory-clothing departed from her, and for the first time, she was "dark" in appearance to Adam. She literally was turned off to Adam! This also meant that for the first time, Adam no longer had communion with the woman's spirit, since it died when she ate the fruit. He looks upon a being which resembles more the creatures of the earth, rather than the pinnacle of God's kingdom.

In that brief moment, Adam has to be asking himself what is happening, nothing looks familiar except for one sign: a hand extended with giving. Despite the loss of her connection to the kingdom of grace, the woman still responds with the characteristic which is the hallmark of the kingdom: the giving hand. Adam, still connected to the kingdom, understood this gesture from a deep personal level. At this moment, Adam had a choice to make: Accept the gift or turn it away, and with it, the very essence which makes him whole. Made in the image and likeness of God, Adam makes the decision that a king of grace always makes: Adam took on sin for his bride.

When you make a claim like this, it shocks people. They have never looked at this matter from that perspective. Certainly, the King of Grace would take on the sins of the world thousands of years later by claiming in a garden that He would follow the will of the Father. If you want to understand the actions of Adam in the Garden of Eden, then you need to understand the actions of Jesus in the Garden of Gethsemane. The last Adam will correct the results from the first Adam.

The Natural Effect

So both the woman and Adam had eaten the fruit which they were forbidden to partake of. The result was immediate death to their spirits, which meant a disconnect from the realm of grace which they were formed and fashioned from. Do we have any idea what that disconnect feels like at this moment? Let me give you

Grace for Shame

two last verses which properly depict what that effect looks and feels like.

> And they **were both naked**, the man and his wife, and **were not ashamed**. – Genesis 2:25

> Then the eyes of both of them were opened, and **they knew that they were naked**; and they sewed fig leaves together and made themselves coverings. – Genesis 3:7

In these two verses, the word "naked" is different in the Hebrew. They both have the same premise, bare or nude, but how you arrived in this condition is what makes the difference and shows us what the effect of the fall had upon the grace they once knew. The first word in verse 2:25 depicts the nakedness which defines a newborn child. The second word defines the nakedness which is associated with a whore, a person who sells themselves to receive a living wage. You will find in the Hebrew language a number of words which have the term "disgrace, reprove or reproach" as one of their meanings. For each of these words, the root meaning is the same: to be made naked, just like Genesis 3:7. Obviously, there is a great sense of shame which comes with the baggage of this form of nakedness.

What we need to be aware of is this: Whenever we feel shame, no matter what the situation, we have experienced the effect of being disconnected from grace. Proverbs tells us that love covers a multitude of sins. This is speaking directly to the nature of the kingdom. Anyone who operates from the kingdom is expected to "cover" another from any potential shame the enemy brings. Realize that Jesus endured the greatest shame known to mankind by being hung on a cross, naked, with the entire weight of the sins of man placed upon him for each and every one of us. This was His grace gift to us so we would be reconnected to the Kingdom of Grace not having to experience the weapon of shame which the enemy uses so effectively.

Finally, what is interesting is their response to having their eyes opened and seeing their nakedness is to immediately work at obtaining a "living" covering to replace what has departed from them. This tells me that the glory which clothed them is a living material which they could sense about them. Because they sewed the fig leaves together, it tells me that the glory clothing is tailored to fit the person exactly. We, in like manner, will be fitted with the clothing the Father has perfected for our eternal purpose.

So in this teaching, we have seen how the enemy was a cherub created to protect God in worship and was expelled from the Kingdom of Grace due to his pride and covetousness. He devised a plan to regain the position he sought after and used the highest expression of God's creation, the woman, to usurp the kingdom from the man. We have seen how the enemy uses doubt to work with circumstances in order to undermine your faith or belief. Also, in this we have revealed (no pun intended) what the disconnect from grace looks like and the emotional condition of shame which results from it.

2.2 The Shame of It All

(26) And God said, Let us make man in our image, after our likeness: and let them have dominion over the fish of the sea, and over the fowl of the air, and over the cattle, and over all the earth, and over every creeping thing that creepeth upon the earth. (27) So God created man in his own image, in the image of God created he him; male and female created he them.
– Genesis 1:26-27

Created on the sixth day, the man and the woman came into "being" in the image and likeness of the Father. This is an important distinction to recognize in the original intent of man: Their appearance was like that of God. When He looked at them, He saw Himself. When the man and the woman looked at each other, they saw God. There was nothing that they had to "do" to try to be an image of God because this is how they naturally presented themselves one to another. Ask yourself these two questions: 1) does the Creator of all things see Himself when He looks at me, and 2) do I see Him when I look at another person? Your inability to answer yes to each of these questions reflects an image which is different than the original intent the Father has for your life, and it may be the indication that you are hampered by shame.

The man and the woman in a shame-less existence spent their first entire day in a posture of rest with the Father observing the Sabbath. During this day, they experienced the celebration of worshipping the Father of all grace in the very creation He designed for them. During this time, they were given the opportunity to partake of the vast splendor of the kingdom which had been granted to them in the very presence of the Creator.

Sometime after the Sabbath day had occurred, we are confronted with the events found in Chapter 3 of Genesis: the fall of man. The enemy of the Kingdom of Grace deceives the woman into taking of the forbidden fruit from the tree of the knowledge of good and evil. We pick this up in verse 6,

> *(6) So when the woman saw that the tree was good for food, that it was pleasant to the eyes, and a tree desirable to make one wise, she took of its fruit and ate. She also gave to her husband with her, and he ate. (7) Then the eyes of both of them were opened, **and they knew that they were naked**; and they sewed fig leaves together and made **<u>themselves coverings</u>**. (8) And they heard the sound of the LORD God walking in the garden in the cool of the day, and Adam and his wife hid themselves from the presence of the LORD God among the trees of the garden. (9) Then the LORD God called to Adam and said to him, "Where are you?" (10) So he said, "I heard Your voice in the garden, and **<u>I was afraid because I was naked; and I hid myself."</u>** (11) And He said, **<u>"Who told you that you were naked?</u>** Have you eaten from the tree of which I commanded you that you should not eat?" (12) Then the man said, **<u>"The woman whom You gave to be with me, she gave me of the tree, and I ate."</u>** – Genesis 3:6-12*

Notice in verse 7 of this passage that once their eyes are open and they have the sense that they are naked, they began doing something to give them an identity which they believe corresponds to their previous condition. This is the human reaction to shame: Having been exposed and left vulnerable, I need to cover myself and/or hide. Yet what is the response from the Father when the man admits that he was naked and he hid himself from God? "Who told you that you were naked?"

Now recall that I previously stated that this term of naked is in the category of what we call today as a harlot or prostitute—one who chooses to obtain a monetary gain in exchange for a creative intimate interlude with as many participants as the financial need demands. To bring a greater understanding as to this term, the Hebrew characterizes this type of harlot as a temple prostitute. This person, who acted as the earthly representative for the fertility gods in the region, would engage in sexual acts as a form of worship. In order to obtain the blessing of those gods, such as provision, favorable weather, or healthy livestock, a participant would come to these prostitutes and present a token as an offering in exchange for the sexual service that they provided, which was believed to release the favor of the gods. These transactions and their associated acts were always conducted in full public viewing, generally at the highest location in the region so that the affects of the acts, or blessing, could be experienced by the entire region.

Therefore, when the text in verse 7 states, "...that they knew they were naked..." it's not simply saying that they looked down and saw that they had no clothes on. It is telling us they realized that their action had resulted in a value exchange between how God created them and what the enemy desired for them. In essence, they had exchanged their worship for a god who satisfied, or elevated, their humanity. This is why the Father asks, "Who said you were naked?" The Father does not answer to the humanity where they are speaking from. We often ask God to validate our humanity when He has already defined our destiny according to His deity.

Understand that God's word creates. If God said to the man, "You are naked. How did this happen?" man would forever be "naked" and any explanation would be mute. The declaration "You are..." creates. Now I realize this might be an elementary lesson in understanding God's word, but most people fail to see the significance of it in God's question to Adam. If man is formed in the image and likeness of God, then like God, man has the same creative power in his words. God's question is to put in focus a principle of authority: If two or more agree on a matter, it is so.

Adam's declaration of his condition pertains to him in his place of dominion. It is a creative word waiting for agreement. God gave dominion to man on this planet, which means that man is in the first position of

HOW OFTEN HAVE YOU USED THE PHRASE, "YOU ARE . . ." TO CREATE SOMETHING THAT YOU DIDN'T WANT IN YOUR LIFE?

authority. God can only act on earth when man comes in agreement with Him. Notice I didn't say that God can only act when He agrees with man. Man must agree with God and his kingdom in order for God to work on the earth. Since God never intended or saw man "naked," He will not agree with the declaration of man in his humanity. Since there is no agreement, the man's word does not have the ability to create its expression on the earth.

And please note, we have no record that the woman came into a verbal agreement with Adam's declaration. Even though they both

Grace for Shame

experienced the effect of eating from the tree, man was the only one to verbally declare its result. The woman, therefore knowing their condition, kept it to herself. Welcome to the dual actions of shame. Most will keep quiet about the condition of their actions so as not to draw attention to themselves. Others will be more vocal, actually seeking agreement with others for their condition.

That last statement might seem a bit bizarre considering the nature we're dealing with. But consider the absurd question which people often respond to their actions with: "Have you no shame?" Do they want to declare that an amount of shame should exist or shouldn't exist? Remember that the principle of agreement is at work, and these people want to be validated in their humanity. This validation is known as the fruit of knowledge.

2.3 The Ugly Trio

Shame on you!

I am so ashamed to be seen in public with you!

What a shame!

How can you think of such shameful things about me?

It's a crying shame!

Have you heard or expressed one of these sayings? I know that I have, and it wasn't until I began this study that I even considered what I was pronouncing. Revelation has a way of changing your use of language.

I'm going to make an assumption here. If you've read this far, you've been waiting to find out how shame is dealt with by grace. While what you've read so far has been good (and maybe useful), you've been impacted in some way by the nature of shame, and you're looking for some way to get through or over the effects which it has exploded on your life. Is this a secure assumption on my part? If it's not for you, then please continue reading, realizing I'm going to be talking to those who fit this assumption.

If you've ever had the pleasure of going crab fishing, there is a unique process which occurs with crabs once they are caught and put into a bucket or holding tank. Periodically, one of the crabs will make an attempt to try to escape the confines of the bucket by moving towards the top of the bucket. Just as this crab struggles and fights to rise to the top by clawing through all the other crabs, the point comes when there is no more fighting needed to make the stretch towards freedom. It is at this moment as the crab stretches forth to grasp onto the rim when the few crabs below it will also reach up. But they don't reach up for freedom; they reach up and pull the crab back down into the bucket where it must again fight and struggle towards freedom. This is a picture of how shame operates in the lives of so many people.

I'm going to step away from the kingdom message for a moment in order to provide you with an understanding of this topic as viewed from the world's perspective. My purpose for this is because many of our "shame" encounters first occurred in this arena, and they have clung to us like crabs in a bucket all this time. So let's see how the world defines and measures what I call the ugly trio: shame, the emotions of humiliation, and embarrassment which accompanies it.

Shame

According to *Webster's Dictionary,* shame is defined as:

SHAME, n. (1.) A painful sensation excited by a consciousness of guilt, or of having done something which injures reputation; or by of that which nature or modesty prompts us to conceal. Shame is particularly excited by the disclosure of actions which, in the view of men, are mean and degrading. Hence it is often or always manifested by a downcast look or by blushes, called confusion of face; (2). The cause or reason of shame; that which brings reproach, and degrades a person in the estimation of others. Thus an idol is called a shame; (3.) Reproach; ignominy; derision; contempt. (4.) The parts which modesty requires to be covered; (5.) Dishonor; disgrace.

SHAME, v.t. 1. To make ashamed; to excite a consciousness of guilt or of doing something derogatory to reputation; to cause to blush; (2.)To disgrace; (3.) To mock at.

SHAME, v.i. To be ashamed.

Some of the synonyms for shame are disgrace, dishonor, disrepute, infamy, ignominy, and opprobrium, and their meanings are found in the following *Webster's 9th Collegiate Dictionary* entry for shame:

Shame stresses a pain or humiliating disgrace often suffered because of another's act or behavior and often implies feelings of guilt and remorse;

Disgrace implies a loss of favor or esteem once enjoyed or a severe humiliation not necessarily deserved;

Dishonor often equals disgrace but not implied loss of self-esteem;

Disrepute stresses loss of one's good name or the attachment of a bad name or reputation;

Infamy stresses notoriety and well deserved extreme contempt;

Ignominy applies chiefly to the humiliation of defeat or insult usually without implication of moral blame;

Opprobrium adds to disgrace the implication of severe reproach or condemnation

These definitions give us a basic understanding of shame and its use or impact upon the lives of people. Yet from a clinical side, there is more information which can be found. From the *Gale Dictionary of Psychoanalysis*, we discover this entry on shame:

The word shame encompasses: 1) the raw emotion linked to a loss of one's bearings; 2) judgment about this state (the perception of shame as such resulting from the comparison of oneself with a model); and 3) judgment about both this emotion and the possible causes of shame (implying possibilities for action). In all cases, shame is a sense of anxiety about being excluded, that is, not only fear of a withdrawal of love, but even withdrawal of any form of interest.

In "Three Essays on the Theory of Sexuality" (1905), Sigmund Freud linked shame to the action of the forces of repression (what was initially an object of pleasure becomes an object of modesty, disgust, or shame). By contrast, in "La honte comme angoisse sociale" (Shame as a Social Anxiety; 1929), Imre Hermann described shame as a "social anxiety" linked to attachment.

Shame always has two aspects: one relating to individual mental functioning (anxiety about mental disintegration), and the other relating to relations with the group (anxiety about being excluded). Pathological shame is to be distinguished from shame as a signal of alarm. Coping with shame involves both naming it and reinforcing the secondary processes to limit its disintegrative effects. It can be displaced or masked, especially by resignation, anger, guilt, or hate.

To a certain extent, shame was a "blind spot" for Freud and, in his wake, for many psychoanalysts who reduced it to a pathological affect linked to the ideal ego and opposed to the guilt associated with the oedipal superego. However, it is a concept that is essential to the understanding of the dynamics of social bonds (it protects people from engaging in nonhuman actions) and intergenerational secrets.

Wikipedia, the internet encyclopedia, has a great deal to say about shame too. In its entry on the subject, the following is listed:

Shame is, variously, an effect, emotion, cognition, state, or condition. The roots of the word shame are thought to derive from an older word meaning to cover; as such, covering oneself, literally or figuratively, is a natural expression of shame.

The location of the dividing line between the concepts of shame, guilt, and embarrassment is not fully standardized.

According to cultural anthropologist Ruth Benedict, shame is a violation of cultural or social values while guilt feelings arise from violations of one's internal values. Thus, it is possible to feel ashamed of thought or behavior that no one knows about and to feel guilty about actions that gain the approval of others.

Psychoanalyst Helen B. Lewis argued that "The experience of shame is directly about the self, which is the focus of evaluation. In guilt, the self is not the central object of negative evaluation, but rather the thing done is the focus." Similarly, Fossum and Mason say in their book <u>Facing Shame</u> that "While guilt is a painful feeling of regret and responsibility for one's actions, shame is a painful feeling about oneself as a person." Following this line of reasoning, Psychiatrist Judith Lewis Herman concludes that "Shame is an acutely self-conscious state in which the self is 'split,' imagining the self in the eyes of the other; by contrast, in guilt the self is unified."

Clinical psychologist Gershen Kaufman's view of shame is derived from that of Affect Theory, namely that shame is one of a set of instinctual, short-duration physiological reactions to stimulation. In this view, guilt is considered to be a learned behavior consisting essentially of self-directed blame or contempt, with shame occurring consequent to such behaviors making up a part of the overall experience of guilt. Here, self-blame and self-contempt mean the application, towards (a part of) one's self, of exactly the same dynamic that blaming of, and contempt for, others represents when it is applied interpersonally. Kaufman saw that mechanisms such as blame or contempt may be used as a defending strategy against the experience of shame and that someone who has a pattern of applying them to himself may well attempt to defend against a shame experience by applying self-blame or self-contempt. This, however, can lead to an internalized, self-reinforcing sequence of shame events for which Kaufman coined the term "shame spiral".

One view of difference between shame and embarrassment says that shame does not necessarily involve public humiliation while embarrassment does, that is, one can feel shame for an act known only to oneself but in order to be embarrassed one's actions must be revealed to others. In the field of ethics (moral psychology, in particular), however, there is debate as to whether or not shame is a heteronomous emotion, i.e., whether or not shame does involve recognition on the part of the ashamed that they have been judged negatively by others. Immanuel Kant and his followers held that shame is heteronomous; Bernard Williams and others have argued that shame can be autonomous. Shame may carry the connotation of a response to something that is morally wrong whereas embarrassment is the response to something that is morally neutral but socially unacceptable. Another view of shame and embarrassment says that the two emotions lie on a continuum and only differ in intensity.

Shame is considered one aspect of socialization in all societies. According to the anthropologist Ruth Benedict, cultures may be classified by their emphasis on the use of either shame or guilt to regulate the social activities of individuals. Shared opinions and expected behaviours and potential associated feelings of shame are in any case proven to be effective in guiding behaviour of a group or society.

Shame may be used by those people who commit relational aggression and may occur in the workplace as a form of overt social control or aggression. Shaming is also a central feature of punishment, shunning, or ostracism. In addition, shame is often seen in victims of child neglect and child abuse.

Before we proceed in looking deeper into this matter, we need to address two more mentioned terms associated with the process of shame; these are humiliation and embarrassment.

Humiliation

American Heritage Dictionary describes humiliation as:

1. The act of humiliating; degradation.
2. The state of being humiliated or disgraced; shame.
3. A humiliating condition or circumstance.

Wikipedia's entry for the subject of humiliation contains the following information:

Humiliation (also called stultification) is the abasement of pride, which creates mortification or leads to a state of being humbled or reduced to lowliness or submission. It can be brought about through bullying, intimidation, physical or mental mistreatment or trickery, or by embarrassment if a person is revealed to have committed a socially or legally unacceptable act. Whereas humility can be sought alone as a means to de-emphasise the ego, humiliation must involve other person(s), though not necessarily directly or willingly. Acting to humiliate yourself may be linked to a personal belief (as with mortification of the flesh, with some religions), or it can be part of erotic humiliation where the belittling activity provides emotional and/or sexual arousal or heightened sensation.

Humiliation is currently an active research topic, and is now seen as an important - and complex - core dynamic in human

Grace for Shame

relationships, having implications at intrapersonal, interpersonal, institutional and international levels.

Punishment or Interrogation Tactic

Forced humiliation of Jews in Nazi Germany. Humiliation of one person by another (the humiliator) is often used as a way of asserting power over them, and is a common form of oppression, bullying or abuse used in a police, military, or prison context during legal interrogations or illegal torture sessions. Many now-obsolete public punishments were deliberately designed to be humiliating, e.g. tarring and feathering lawbreakers, pillory, "mark of infamy" (stigma) as a means of "making an example" of a person and presenting a deterrent to others. Some of the states in America have experimented with humiliating or shaming lawbreakers by publishing their names and indicating their offense (e.g., with soliciting prostitutes or drinking and driving). The Chinese government routinely humiliates lawbreakers by parading them in public with a sign around their neck indicating their offense. Humiliation activities such as stripping a prisoner naked or having them simulate sex acts are often contrary to policies in police or prison settings. Nevertheless, these humiliation tactics have been used by secret police and military interrogators as a way of eliciting cooperation or breaking down the resistance of a prisoner.

A Wider Human Perspective

Donald Klein described humiliation as "a powerful factor in human affairs that has, for a variety of reasons, been overlooked by students of individual and collective behavior. It is a pervasive and all too destructive influence in the behavior of individuals, groups, organizations, and nations." That statement captures the degree to which humiliation affects our lives, ranging from the deeply personal right up to global levels.

Even though it is a subjective emotion, it has a universal aspect which applies to all human beings: "it is the feeling of being put down, made to feel less than one feels oneself to be." This feeling can be felt as an individual (as when one feels offended by another) or as a community, group or nation.

Feelings of humiliation can produce 'humiliated fury' which, when turned inward can result in apathy and depression, and when turned outward can give rise to paranoia, sadistic behaviour and fantasies of revenge. Klein explains, "When it is outwardly directed, humiliated fury unfortunately creates additional victims, often including innocent bystanders .... When it is inwardly directed, the resulting self-hate renders victims incapable of meeting their own needs, let alone having energy available to love and care for others." He goes on to say, "In either case, those who are consumed by humiliated fury are absorbed in themselves or their cause, wrapped in wounded pride..."

Not all acts of humiliation are intentional. They can be committed quite accidentally. Sometimes, feelings of humiliation can arise simply because of misunderstandings.

Because these feelings can have very destructive consequences, ranging from interpersonal conflict to international terrorism, Lindner has called them the "nuclear bomb of the emotions." With an awareness of the emotional power created by humiliation, those feelings can - albeit with considerable effort - be turned into a force for constructive action, as exemplified by people such as Gandhi or Nelson Mandela.

Embarrassment

American Heritage Dictionary provides us with the following definition of embarrassment:

1. The act or an instance of embarrassing.
2. The state of being embarrassed.
3. A source or cause of being embarrassed.

4. An overabundance: an embarrassment of choices at a buffet dinner; an embarrassment of riches.

Wikipedia's material on embarrassment is diverse, so I'm only going to provide you with some of its content for the sake of space.

Embarrassment is an emotional state experienced upon having a socially or professionally unacceptable act or condition witnessed by or revealed to others. Usually some amount of loss of honor or dignity is involved, but how much and the type depends on the embarrassing situation. It is similar to shame, except that shame may be experienced for an act known only to oneself. Also, embarrassment usually carries the connotation of being caused by an act that is merely socially unacceptable, rather than morally wrong.

Causes

The science of embarrassment is called emderatology. Emderatology is a technique often used by employers to examine the way their employees deal with this. Embarrassment can be personal, caused by unwanted attention to private matters or personal flaws or mishaps. Some causes of embarrassment stem from personal actions, such as being caught in a lie or in making a mistake, losing badly in a competition, getting debagged, or being caught performing bodily functions such as flatulence. In many cultures, being seen nude or inappropriately dressed is a particularly stressful form of embarrassment (see modesty). Personal embarrassment could also stem from the actions of others which place the embarrassed person in a socially awkward situation, such as having one's awkward baby pictures shown to friends, having someone make a derogatory comment about one's appearance or behaviour, discovering one is the victim of gossip, being rejected by another person (see also humiliation), being made the focus of attention (e.g. birthday celebrants, newlyweds), or even witnessing someone else's embarrassment.

Personal embarrassment is usually accompanied by some combination of blushing, sweating, nervousness, stammering, and fidgeting. Sometimes the embarrassed person will try to mask embarrassment with smiles or nervous laughter, especially in etiquette situations; such a response is more common in certain cultures, which may lead to misunderstanding. There may also be feelings of anger depending on the perceived seriousness of the situation, especially if the individual thinks another person is intentionally causing the embarrassment. There is a range of responses, with the most minor being a perception of the embarrassing act as inconsequential or even humorous, to intense apprehension or fear.

The idea that embarrassment serves an apology or appeasement function originated with Goffman (1967) who argued the embarrassed individual "demonstrates that he/she is at least disturbed by the fact and may prove worthy at another time". Semin & Manstead (1982) demonstrated social functions of embarrassment whereby the perpetrator of knocking over a sales display (the 'bad act') was deemed more likable by others if he/she appeared embarrassed than if he/she appeared unconcerned – regardless of restitution behaviour (rebuilding the display). The capacity to experience embarrassment can also be seen to be functional for the group or culture. It has been demonstrated that those who are not prone to embarrassment are more likely to engage in antisocial behaviour – for example, adolescent boys who displayed more embarrassment were found to be less likely to engage in aggressive/delinquent behaviours. Similarly, embarrassment exhibited by boys more likely to engage in aggressive/delinquent behaviour was less than one-third of that exhibited by non-aggressive boys (Ketlner et al. 1995). Thus proneness to embarrassment (i.e. a concern for how one is evaluated by others) can act as a brake on behaviour that would be dysfunctional for group or culture.

Professional Embarrassment

Embarrassment can also be professional or official, especially after statements expressing confidence in a stated course of action, or willful disregard for evidence. Embarrassment increases greatly in instances involving official duties or workplace facilities, large amounts of money or materials, or loss of human life. Examples of causes include a government's failed public policy, exposure of corrupt practices or unethical behaviour, a celebrity whose personal habits receive public scrutiny or face legal action, or officials caught in serious personally embarrassing situations. Even small errors or miscalculations can lead to significantly greater official embarrassment if it is discovered that there was willful disregard for evidence or directives involved (e.g., see Space Shuttle Challenger).

Not all official failures result in official embarrassment, even if the circumstances lead to some slight personal embarrassment for the people involved. For example, losing a close political election might cause some personal embarrassment for the candidate but generally would be considered an honorable loss in the profession and thus not necessarily lead to professional embarrassment. Similarly, a scientist might be personally disappointed and embarrassed if one of his hypotheses was proven wrong, but would not normally suffer professional embarrassment as a result. By contrast, exposure of falsified data supporting a scientific claim (e.g., see Hwang Woo-Suk) would likely lead to professional embarrassment in the scientific community. Professional or official embarrassment is often accompanied by public expressions of anger, denial of involvement, or attempts to minimize the consequences. Sometimes the embarrassed entity will issue press statements, remove or distance themselves from sub-level employees, attempt to carry on as if nothing happened, suffer income loss, emigrate, or completely vanish from public view.

The Spiritual Side of Shame, Embarrassment, and Humiliation

Having seen the world's view on the ugly trio, let's take a look at what the Bible has to say about them. The first mention of shame comes, as I've previous shown, in Genesis 2:25, where the man and the woman were naked in the garden and were not "ashamed." That word for "ashamed" in Hebrew is "bush," and it is a root word having the meaning of:

Properly to pale, that is, by implication to be ashamed; also (by implication) to be disappointed, or delayed: - (be, make, bring to, cause, put to, with, a-) shame (-d), be (put to) confounded (-fusion), become dry, delay, be long.

Since this is a root word, I thought you should know what other words draw from it for their meanings. There are four other words which draw from this word: two which mean shamefulness; one that means the male genitals; and one called "bosheth" that means:

Shame (the feeling and the condition, as well as its cause); by implication (specifically) an idol: - ashamed, confusion, + greatly, (put to) shame (-ful thing).

Before I provide any Scriptures where some of these words appear, I want to draw your attention to the definitions I have provided. Please note that confusion is something associated with shame in both of these definitions. Also see that a delay or disappointment can imply shame. But the most glaring thing is that shame specifically implies an idol. The definition of an idol is:

1. An image, form or representation, usually of a man or other animal, consecrated as an object of worship; a pagan deity. Idols

are usually statues or images, carved out of wood or stone, or formed of metals, particularly silver or gold.
2. An image.
3. A person loved and honored to adoration.
4. Anything on which we set our affections; that to which we indulge an excessive attachment.
5. A representation.

How many times have you experienced shame from someone who you loved or adored and have felt confused by it? Or how often have you seen someone who held a high level of esteem in public have a shameful incident which confounds those that established them in their place of influence? Stay with me for a moment more before I go into the Scriptures.

Let's take a look at humiliation. The word "humiliate" or "humiliation" is not found in the traditional King James interpretation of the Bible, but this doesn't mean that they're not there. If you go to the Hebrew text, you will find them in a couple of different words. The root word is "kâna," and it has the meaning to bend the knee, to humiliate, vanquish, to bring into subjection, to subdue, to bring low. I trust you can see that its meaning is dealing with the defeat which occurs in a battle between foes. Another word which means humiliated has "kâna" as it root, and it is the word "kena'an." This word also has the meaning of merchant and traffic. In case you can't make out the phonetic rendering of this word, then maybe it may help if you knew this is the word Canaan, the son of Ham, Noah's grandson, and the person which the land of Canaan, or what is possibly more familiar to you as the Promised Land, was named after.

Embarrass is not rendered in the Bible in either the Hebrew or the Greek, but this doesn't mean that it is not evident in action. The word itself has a unique etymology having transversed the European continent over many centuries, but its first use possibly is of Portuguese origin, where it was meant as a noose, a rope to halt. The prefix "em" for this word in the old English means "in." So apparently someone is in the noose. When I was studying this word, I was led to this passage which I believe accurately depicts what embarrassment represents.

> *(4) So shall the king of Assyria lead away the Egyptians prisoners, and the Ethiopians captives, young and old, naked and barefoot, **even with their buttocks uncovered**, to the shame of Egypt. – Isaiah 20:4*

During the days that this passage reflects, the victor would often parade the naked conquered prisoners, tied together with a rope about their necks, through the land as a show of their great might. The population of the land they were moving through viewed these demonstrations as a warning of the ability of the victor to subdue his subjects, and should any feel impassioned to rise up, they knew that similar treatment would befall them for their quest. Yet even in this, there is still a deeper meaning, and it's time to explore all of these items together to see the full spiritual implications.

History Defining Nakedness

I have stated previously that the first mention of shame found in the Bible is found in Genesis 2:25, and it is associated with the nakedness of the man and the woman. Some of you are probably getting tired of me mentioning this, but it has a very significant meaning in the kingdom as you are about to see. Additionally, I have stated that the fall produced a form of nakedness, which is commonly associated with a temple prostitute and is diametrically opposite to the nakedness found in Genesis 2:25. So let me ask you this question, and if you can answer it correctly, it will have the seeds of understanding the spiritual aspects of shame: If Adam and the woman were the only two people on the face of the earth at the time of the fall, why would their nakedness be compared to a temple prostitute—a position which never comes onto the scene for at least another 1500 years?

MANY BELIEVE THAT THE TERM "BEFORE THE LORD" IS A POSITIVE THING. IN THE CASE OF NIMROD, IT MEANT THAT HIS ACTIONS WERE SO OFFENSIVE THAT GOD HAD TO SEE WHAT CAUSED HIM TO DO SUCH THINGS.

The first five books of the Bible are known as the books of Moses to the Hebrews. Four of those books take a sort of biographical direction in depicting how God, through Moses, dealt with the children of Israel in their exodus out of Egypt and travels into the Promised Land. Genesis is the history of Israel prior to Moses, so it draws from the historical record given by the oral traditions of the people in the region and the inspiration of God's Spirit. I mention this simply because it is Moses under the guidance of the Holy Spirit who has described the nakedness of man after the fall, a description which was very evident in the land which Moses came from and the children of Israel were to settle in. Moses draws this description for the actions which transpired not with Adam but with a fellow known as Nimrod, the great-grandson of Noah.

(6) And the sons of Ham; Cush, and Mizraim, and Phut, and Canaan. (7) And the sons of Cush; Seba, and Havilah, and

Sabtah, and Raamah, and Sabtecha: and the sons of Raamah;
Sheba, and Dedan. (8) And Cush begat Nimrod: he began to be
a mighty one in the earth. (9) He was a mighty hunter before
the LORD: wherefore it is said, Even as Nimrod the mighty
hunter before the LORD. (10) And the beginning of his kingdom
was Babel, and Erech, and Accad, and Calneh, in the land of
Shinar. – Genesis 10:6-10

This is all that the biblical record mentions about Nimrod, yet the historical record from the rabbinical teachings and the cuneiform writings from the region in those days depict a very interesting picture of the man. The rabbis tell us that the description in verse 9 is not as pleasing as one might think it to mean. The term "before the Lord" actually means that because of the actions which he took, he was continually before the Lord, similar to how a stubborn child is always at the attention of his parents. The claim of being a mighty hunter was two-fold in its implications: He was a protector of the people from the great skills which he displayed in taking down the animals that preyed on the people, and he was a great warrior that began to battle the surrounding communities and brought them into his subjection. He was the first recorded individual to declare himself as a king (v. 10), building high-walled fortified cities as a symbol of an empire which began in Babel and would later become the center of the Babylonian Empire. The rabbis claim Nimrod was one who would drape himself in robes of piety to deceive the masses and that he ensnared people with his words, inciting them to rebel against God.

Nowhere was this last act more evident than in the building of the tower of Babel, which is found in Genesis 11. Built some 350 years after the flood, the historical record claims the purpose of the tower was to create a platform that the waters would never ascend to and a place where Nimrod could battle God! It appears that Nimrod took great exception to the flood, and he vowed to see that God would never perform such an act again. The construction of the tower was conducted in such a fashion that the bricks themselves were assembled in a manner to be waterproof. Even after the confusion of the tongues of the people building the tower, history tells us the entire tower and the city of Babel survived until about the time of Alexander the Great, when his legions toppled the structure and surrounding buildings.

Further records also claim Nimrod used the tower to worship the sun and began making sacrifices to the sun. In these proceedings, Nimrod became the priest to the sun god, eventually elevating himself even higher and taking on the new name of Baal, which means master or husband. The historic anthropological records claim that in the dispersal of the people, they took these ceremonies which were conducted at the tower site with them into the new territories where they commuted to, explaining why so many of the world's religious ceremonies share common themes.

Many years later, another ruler, a woman named Sumeris, would arise in the same land of Nimrod. While adhering to the tenets of Baal worship, she would institute an additional ritual for the worship of the moon god, Ashtoreth. These ceremonies would encompass the worship of Baal and his "wife," Ashtoreth, who had been elevated to fertility gods throughout the surrounding region, which encompassed the areas from the Euphrates River to the Nile River and included the land of Canaan.

The rituals for worshipping these idols varied greatly due to the needs of the people, but common acts were human sacrifice, often children, and sexual acts conducted by virgins, prostitutes, and those designated priests representing the various idols. The Baal idols were often made from stone, while the Ashtoreth idols were trees or poles which were placed at the highest places in the community as a depiction of the tower of Babel.

This brief understanding of the development of idol worship is vital if you are to comprehend what the description of naked means to Moses when he claims this to be the condition of Adam and the woman in Genesis 3. The greatest shame of mankind was displayed in Nimrod's actions of believing that he alone could battle God and then elevating himself into that very position. How humiliating it must have been for the people around him who were forced to bend their knee in subservience to him.

You must consider this very fact: These people were his family members, cousins, aunts, and uncles. These people knew his father and grandfather too, possibly even having spoken to them in person. They knew the story of the flood, just as Nimrod did, and all the acts which God did. They understood the blessing that God had pronounced upon Noah and his sons for them to be fruitful and multiply. And yet the one promise which God made to the entire planet and signified in the sky by a rainbow was forgotten, or just plain ignored, out of the pride that would make Nimrod a deliverer to his "people."

It is these thoughts and actions of one person which influenced the course of humanity away from the relationship which God intended. Yes, I'm speaking of both Adam and Nimrod. In Adam, we see the result of shame from deception by another, while in

Nimrod we see the shame which comes from the deception of exaltation.

Shame, as depicted in the Bible, is always associated with the worship of an idol. Its depiction of nakedness, as someone who offers themselves to a stranger for monetary gain, is consistent with the practices that other idol worshippers performed. The humiliation which comes from a shameful act indicates that the knee has been bowed to a desire which had exalted itself.

I want to make a special note regarding embarrassment here. One of the repeating themes in the discussion on embarrassment has to do with the act of blushing. As we know, blushing is the rush of blood to the face during times of stress, causing the skin to temporarily turn various shades of red. The rabbinical teachings have a rich discourse on the "shedding of blood," and any act which produces the effect described as blushing would be considered as shedding blood. I want you to consider this view: The New Testament declares that we are the temple of God and that we have been made clean by the blood of Jesus. Yet each time we feel the rush of blood to our face, we are shedding "strange" blood in a holy place—an act which could be viewed as a form of sacrifice to an idol. I'm not claiming here that you are doing this intentionally, but merely that the enemy is using the opportunity to defile the temple of God.

> COULD YOUR BLUSHING BE INTERPRETED AS "SHEDDING STRANGE BLOOD?" ACCORDING TO PAUL YOU'RE NOW THE TEMPLE OF GOD SANCTIFIED BY THE BLOOD OF JESUS.

These are just some of the things which God had to prepare for when considering our redemption. There could not be one thing left out which would not be covered in the work Jesus did for us. What we may have not considered is that every act that has shame, humiliation or embarrassment as a motive has been fully covered by the work which is found in the ultimate tool in the Kingdom of God. Before divulging this tool, we need to look at some relevant situations that display the reign of shame in society today.

2.4 The Fruit of Knowledge

Shame is social. Its purpose is to restrain. Shame exists where there is a divergence. Knowledge is the demarcation of divergence.

Both Adam and the woman ate from the tree of the knowledge of good and evil. The result is that mankind has been possessed with the desire to know—not in the sense of knowing someone in a relational manner, which is how the Hebrew interpret the word "know," but in the sense of having a mental, or intellectual, command of a topic, which is the manner that the Greeks interpret the word "know." The distinction in these two understandings can be demonstrated in how you answer this question: Do you know God? On the one hand, do you have a personal relationship with God which is active daily, not just when you need him to fix your mess? Or do you have knowledge of what is required of you to access His "good graces" so your mess can be redeemed?

This latter recognition of "knowing" God has fostered the apparatus of shame's reward system: Am I being, or have I been, good or bad? Notice the reward system doesn't operate on the spectrum of evil simply because we never believe that we are evil creatures. Certainly we can recall people who might have been evil, but as for us, that is just not possible! So we operate shame from a reward system which moves in shades of good, just to the point where it's not recognized as good anymore but just not evil. This system is more commonly called "comparison," and it is the foremost driver of shame.

You don't measure up. On a scale of 1 to 10, you're a 7. If you were more like your brother, sister, father mother, etc... You're not qualified. You're over qualified. Do you like the blue one or the red one? These are some of the most typical references to the act of comparison. There are many other instances where comparison is operating, and you possibly can recall the language better than I. The point I'm trying to make here has do with what is the purpose of comparison.

You are not like me, just as I am not like you. It really is too bad that you are not like me, though, because then I wouldn't have to consider what I'm going to say next because you would already know. As a matter of fact, if you were more like me, then we wouldn't have so many troubles communicating at all. Also, we would like to do the same things together. If you were more like me, then I could trust you better, since I know you wouldn't make such a fool of yourself in front of my friends. If you were more like me, you clearly wouldn't dress like you do or even keep your hair the way you do. I obviously am of a far superior class of individual than you are, and there can be no way of you ever reaching my high status in society. Please, for the common good of all humanity, just crawl under a rock and die!

Comparison, in any form, has one purpose: to force a new identity upon a uniquely defined being.

Comparison can be thrust upon us by others or employed by ourselves. The greater the desire is to adopt a new identity, the greater the potential to use shame, humiliation, and embarrassment to achieve the change. You are unique, and you were created that way so you could fulfill a destiny which only you are capable of fulfilling. Trying to complete that destiny identified as someone else is like having the Easter bunny deliver Christmas presents. Yet we compare people relentlessly so that they will align to our perception of reality.

> DECLARING THAT YOU ARE A "GOOD" PERSON OR THAT YOUR ACTIONS WERE "GOOD" IS STILL OPERATING FROM THE TREE OF THE KNOWLEDGE OF GOOD AND EVIL. ITS FRUIT IS STILL DEATH.
>
> KINGDOM PEOPLE HAVE ETERNAL LIFE. DOING GOOD WITHOUT GOD PRODUCES DEATH.

Judge not, that ye be not judged.
– Matthew 7:1

Good and evil are comparisons, judgments. Most people, when they get married, recite vows of their fidelity towards one another, such as "In sickness and in health and for better and for worse..." Comparison in this instance would mean, "In sickness or health; for better or worse." This would give each person the option of leaving should a change occur which didn't meet their liking. (Oh, that seems to be the prevailing mode today!)

What is your net worth?

Shame reduces your net worth. It defaces the value which has been placed upon you. Shame, embarrassment and humiliation all produce an effacing effect on your destiny.

Net worth is determined in business matters by deducting your liabilities from your assets. As an example, let's say you have liabilities totaling $500 and assets equaling $800; your net worth would equal $300 ($800 - $500 = $300). The $300 is a set value that is your reward for your business transactions. Shame, in this example, affects the $300 by reducing its value. Some might think that shame, embarrassment and humiliation are counted in your liabilities, but you must recognize that they attack your value as a person, not who you are as a person.

Value as a person is related to your ability to conduct your affairs with another with all your weaknesses (liabilities) and strengths (assets) in operation. If you were stranded on deserted island by yourself, your value is very low with no other person with which to interact. This scenario in business would be known as building your portfolio (assets). If you were stranded with another person, your value climbs dramatically since you provide a means of support and/or protection for them, just as they do for you.

So let's assume the two of you have just been stranded. The value that each of you have is high. The first thing you both decide to do is build a fire and set about gathering the materials you need. Since you have no matches or other advanced methods of igniting the tinder, you're both required to start the fire using a method employing friction that is laborious, like rubbing two sticks together.

Given that you're both novices to this technique, you both share the responsibility of attempting to start the fire over a period of many hours. Physically and emotionally exhausted, you finally generate an ember from your works and begin nursing it with small amounts of tinder trying to coax it into a flame. You ask your associate to hand you more tinder, and as they rise to get it, they kick a small amount of dirt on top of the ember you've just made. Despite that both of you have worked arduously to produce this ember, in frustration you lash out verbally against your forlorn collaborator. Has the net worth of either of you changed? Has the value you have for each other changed?

Shame, embarrassment and humiliation always affect our value towards another. Shame devalues us in the eyes of another, while embarrassment and humiliation devalue us in our own eyes.

If we return back to the business model explanation, where there is net worth of $300, and combine it with these two stranded people, we'll be able to better understand what transpires. Say that shame, embarrassment and humiliation have an inflationary effect of $100 each. I call it an inflationary effect because these three emotions most often occur when passions are inflamed.

When you both landed on the island, each of you had a net worth value of $300 towards each other. Throughout the entire fire building operation, those values never wavered until the fatal moment you lashed out at your cohort. Your diatribe activates the shame card, which reduces their value by $100 to a total of $200 in their continuing relationship with you. The significance of their actions is not lost on them activating both the embarrassment and humiliation card at $100 each, reducing their own perceived value to a total of $100. But notice this: If they also feel a sense of shame for what was done, they now have a total value of zero, or in other words, they feel worthless.

Now a whole new dynamic in the relationship exists. You value them at $200, while they believe themselves to be worthless, and they value you still at $300. As transactions continue to take place in the relationship, you notice that the output of the person has reduced remarkably from the beginning, and you wonder what is going on with them. You confront them about it, and they offer some explanation which just doesn't make sense to you. What is happening?

Their sense of worthlessness is affecting their ability to produce their natural results. Your diminished view of their worth to you has created in you a sense of greater value without actually increasing your net worth. This is an effect of shame too. When its web is cast upon another, it entangles the one who cast it too. Consider that this confrontation may activate any one part of the ugly trio and reduce again their own perceived value now into the loss category. Once in this situation, they will find it next to impossible to point out a matter of shame in you, because they feel so bankrupt that no value is added to them in doing so.

This is partly an explanation of why battered women remain with their abusers, alcoholics continue to drink, gamblers can't walk away, rape victims can't face their perpetrator, drug addicts find it difficult to kick the habit, and yes, prostitutes can't leave the streets. Yes, I understand that what I've just said could be interpreted as an over-simplification for people whose lives are very diverse. I'm not here to make some clinical diagnosis about their actions, but I simply want to point out the effect that shame, embarrassment and humiliation have produced in their own perceived value. Each one of them, each one of us all, has value.

It did not cost God anything to create the universe, but it cost Him everything to redeem each of us. Your value to Him is beyond any perception which you have about yourself. Even if you feel bankrupt, there are riches beyond comprehension accounted towards you. This is why the enemy has placed his sights on you—not because of some special ability you have, but because your value to the Father is priceless.

2.5 The Reality of Shame

As every man hath received the gift, even so minister the same one to another, as good stewards of the manifold grace of God.
– 1 Peter 4:10

The more you become acquainted with and begin to operate in the realm of the Kingdom of Grace you will soon discover a richness to the realm that before may never have crossed your thoughts: Each person is a facet of God's grace waiting to be unveiled. Stop here for a moment and repeat this statement out loud to yourself:

I am a facet of God's grace that needs to be revealed to the world.

This is not some "feel good" statement designed to motivate you into a better day than yesterday. It is a kingdom truth. Understand that truth does not need you to validate it. Truth will always exist independent of you or me. When we accept and embrace a truth, Jesus said that that truth will make you free or liberate you from the bondage of the previous thoughts which kept you tied. This means every lie has chains which shackle you to it so you will be enslaved to its deceptions. Shame is a lie that has tied many in this world to its deceptive, manipulating and controlling practices, making those victims of it live well below the full measure which the Kingdom of Grace intends for us to live.

Consider the ramifications of this truth of being a facet of God's grace. If you want to experience the fullness of God's grace in your life, you will need to meet every person on the face of the planet so they may impart their specific grace gifting to you. Wherever you may be reading this, there is a person on the other side of the room or even on the other side of the globe, who has a gift for you, just as you have one for them. Yet shame, and its attending emotions of embarrassment and humiliation, will affect both of you in the transference of the gift.

The Social Impact of Shame

I want to take a moment to address the specter of shame which is presently affecting the globe. There is not any area of society that isn't touched by this menace: Political leaders and the nations they operate in; business executives; clergy; teachers; police and firefighters; fathers, mothers, and children. Its tentacles are stretched out wide, and they seem to tighten the most around those who try to rise. The media is its weapon of choice; the internet, newsprint, television, and radio are the fastest purveyors of declaring shame while neglecting their own perpetrating actions in the process.

Two such individuals, Governor Arnold Schwarzenegger and Dominic Strauss Kahn, are people that I want to use as an example, knowing this it will cause some stirring in many people's emotions. Before you read further, please make a mental note about your reactions to each of these people if you know anything about their situation, because it will be revealing how the specter of shame works. I'm not here to judge either of these men's decisions and actions, but I want merely to show you how shame works in halting the efforts of people. A brief explanation of why I chose these two men.

Governor Schwarzenegger, in the spring of 2011, admitted to fathering a child over a decade prior, while he was still married to his wife. Additionally, he provided support to the child while married to his wife. This revelation came a few weeks after Governor Schwarzenegger left his office to a new governor, and the couple officially separated.

Dominic Strauss Kahn, known as DSK in his home country of France, was the head of the International Monetary Fund (IMF) when in the spring of 2011 in New York City, he was arrested for allegedly raping a maid at the hotel in which he was staying and then trying to leave the country. The subsequent trial for Mr. Kahn found him innocent, and the integrity of the maid's testimony became the main point of contention, leading many in the news community to investigate her other actions prior to the incident. Mr. Kahn was permitted to return to his home in France, where another woman made similar accusations about him from years past.

Each of these men is a facet of God's grace. Despite what you many feel about them, recognize that like you, "...God so loved the world that he gave...," and according to Romans 11:29, "...the gifts and calling of God *are* without repentance." Each of these men has a gift which shame has halted or made ineffective independent of whether they are believers or not. "What gift?" you may ask.

Governor Schwarzenegger, previously an international recognized movie actor, held the highest political office in the State of California. While many discount the role of a state governor, this particular political position has great potential for the person who has occupied it. The reason is simple: California is the sixth largest economy in the world. I did not say in the United States, but the world. There is a considerable gifting required to steer such a large economic power. How equipped are you to address the many demands that this position demands?

The International Monetary Fund (IMF) is responsible for lending monies in countries dealing with the effect of market conditions upon their populous. Mr. Kahn was the head of the international organization responsible for transacting trillions of dollars across multiple borders and differing political ideologies. Mr. Kahn was also considered by many in France and abroad to be the lead candidate for the next presidential election to be held in France in 2012. What gifting he would have brought to that nation as a president will not soon be seen, since the events which have occurred to him have derailed his political aspirations. Even his post as head of the IMF has been lost in the wake of the allegations put against him.

The giftings, the insights, and the political perspective which these two men possess have been halted due to the shame that they have each had to experience. Considering the current economic state of the world, their insight will never be entertained since it carries with it the hushed tones of "how could he know what to do after what he did." Some might even say, *"What a shame that we've lost these two figures..."* Did you catch that?

The Subtle Side of Shame

High profile people like I've just shown are not the only ones dealing with shame. There are many areas I could select to highlight how shame is being used to control the lives of people in society, but I'm going to look at just one: education. While I'll be relating statistical information pertaining to these areas in the United States, it should not be hard to find evidence that similar conditions apply around the globe.

Education

Everyone agrees that education is a good thing. But consider the following information:

- Students graduate from college with an average debt of $24,000; this amount has grown 50% in the past decade.
- Student loan debt has increased 511% since 1999 to over $1 trillion, exceeding credit card debt.
- Price for room and board at schools has doubled since 1982.
- Tuitions have risen 439% since 1982.
- Most private schools tuition exceeds $50,000 per year.
- Most grants and scholarships in private schools have been replaced by loans for lower income students.
- Student debt cannot be expunged through bankruptcy.
- Recent studies have shown that 45% of students make no gains in critical reasoning, thinking skills, or writing ability after two years in school.
- More than 45% of students do not graduate.
- Since 2008, 85% of college grads have moved back in with parents.[2]

---

[2]Each of these statistical bullet points can be verified from a graphical depiction located at http://www.thebestcolleges.org/higher_education_bubble/

Think about the following "worst-case" scenario: Young Billy goes off to college in another state to major in education after his parents were able to secure student loans for him over the next four years. His tuition of $24,000.00 for the year and $9,000.00 for room and board, amounting to $33,000.00 per year, will be offset by $7,000.00 from his temporary janitorial work at the local business park. At the end of his four-year term, Billy graduates with his bachelor's degree and presents his 3.8 GPA credentials to the local job market in order to begin his chosen profession as a teacher. Immediately, Billy discovers his unqualified nature, since the teaching profession will only work with those who have secured a master's degree in the appropriate field of study.

Billy tightens his belt and steps into the educational arena again for a 24-month master's program, having secured another student loan for the $28,000.00 yearly tuition. Having moved into an apartment with a friend, his room and board expenses are met by his part time work at the local deli. While earning his master's degree, Billy meets Jane who is also trying to fill her master's degree requirement to become a student counselor. Their relationship blossoms, and they decide after 12 months of seeing each other regularly that they want to get married after they graduate from school.

A week after both have graduated from school with master's degrees in their chosen fields, they sit down to plan out the date for their wedding. On this day, each has also received notice of their loan balances and payments requirements for the entire school loan they incurred. Billy has a loan debt secured by his parents amounting to $104,000 and a personal debt of $56,000 for a grand total of $160,000. His principal payment alone for the next 10 years will be $1,335.00 a month. The local school district is hiring temporary teachers for the present school term, with a pay of $28,000 a year, which if you extend it out over a twelve month period, will pay him after taxes $1,635.00 per month. This is better than the $26,000 starting pay rate back at the school district of Billy's home town.

Jane's financial picture is a little bit brighter. A portion of her student expenses was covered by a few scholarships, but she took a bit longer to finish her degree programs than Billy did, which added to some of her burden. She walks away from school with a personal debt load totaling $115,000.00 making her monthly principal payment $958.00 over the next 10 years. The school district isn't employing any counselors unfortunately, and her prospects in her chosen field will require her to move three states away, where the starting salary is at $35,000 per year, which is $2,040.00 over 12 months.

After careful consideration of their financial picture, they both rule out the possibility of moving in with one of either set of parents. Billy could work in the same district as Jane on a part-time basis until a vacancy could become available possibly in the next school year. There was the potential for him to also work as a janitor in that district during this same time. They both agree that the possibility of marriage at this time is strong within them, and they'll make a firm date after they learn about what the employment environment is like where Jane is headed. They agree because of their work schedules to meet later in the week to go over things and set a date at that time.

During the week, Jane has had a conversation with her mother who related to her the most recent events which have been happening back home. During this talk, her mother tells her of an outing which she just had with her two young granddaughters from Jane's oldest brother. Her mother's description and the joy which Jane perceived began to pull on an emotional longing to have a child also. When her mother asked how things were going with Billy and her on the wedding, she told her she was anxious to set a date. Her mother's response of, "you better hurry – you're not getting any younger," only intensified the desire to have a child within her.

Billy had his own concerns during the week. While working at the deli, he overheard a customer complaining about how he had been wrecked by his ex-wife. When he married her, he didn't know that she had several thousands of dollars in debt from a previous marriage. The customer stated that had he known beforehand, he would have never married her because as soon as they signed the marriage papers, he began getting hounded from collection agents who claimed they were going to garnish his wages. The customer further stated it took him six months to uncover what they were calling about, but by then the collectors had already gotten a judgment against his wife and were grabbing money wherever they could. When he confronted his wife about the matter, she exploded on him, stormed out of the house, and left him with the bills. He hadn't been able to locate her for the past 3 months.

At the end of the week, Billy and Jane get together to set the date for their wedding. Do I need to continue with this scenario further? It may seem a bit exaggerated, but realize these events have happened to a number of people in the past few years. My question to you is this: can you pick out what I'll call "shame points?"

Obvious Points:

1. Billy is not able to get employment with a bachelor's degree.
2. Billy works at a deli with a bachelor's degree in education.
3. Billy and Jane have a personal debt load out of school.

Not-so-Obvious Points:

1. Billy parents secured the school debt. If Billy doesn't start paying for this loan, the parents are going to get hit with it. They will have already gotten notices from the lenders that payment will commence on a certain date. This will begin the momentum of pressuring Billy to action.
2. Billy's potential income is low. Not considering whether the expense of school was worth the income to be generated in the chosen profession will for years place a burden on Billy that will force him to stay in a work environment "just to pay the bills," which may not be what he wants.
3. Billy follows Jane. Socially, this will dog Billy, because he will make less than Jane, and it will appear that he doesn't have leadership ability.
4. The "need to" syndrome has found Jane. Jane's baby desire, spurred on by mother's comment, will eat at her. Social acceptance in some areas is determined by the number of children you have, the car you drive, the people you relate to, etc. Most of these are attached to a need of relevance or significance, and any lack in one or more areas is a cause of public humiliation in varying degrees.

5. What's mine is yours. Billy's customer has a very real bearing on this scenario. The debts of each of these two will become the property of the other when, and if, they wed, unless some legal agreement is reached prior to the wedding. Even this agreement is a shame point at the beginning of a relationship!

The social contract these two people have with their community is the biggest culprit in the shame points here. They were told by parents and teachers fixated on a past movement that a higher education is good thing for them, but they didn't have the actual facts about what the current education would cost them upon graduation or even if the industry they were training for would still exist 10 years from their graduation. Some of these kids come out of an educational process with a bill which is often greater than the mortgage their parents are paying, and they must succumb to living with their parents, waiting to obtain a job in their chosen field. Because of these debts, many are forced into the work place as servants to a lender and required to work long hours in order to pay down their debt. This "extra" or "long" work cycle reduces the population base of a society since more time must be spent on a career (paying the bills) rather than raising a family (paying a different set of bills). As a population base shrinks, those jobs which cater to the young begin to diminish. This effect ripples through the economy as an aging population advances and the past social programs which were engineered towards a certain growth in population begin to feel the pressure of a smaller pool of providers.

I acknowledge that this may be a bit extreme to some of you putting a "worldly" example as subject matter in a "spiritual" book. Don't think for a moment I'm against education; you're reading this book to educate yourself! The Word tells us to get wisdom, to have it be the first thing to obtain, and with wisdom, to get understanding. But there is a difference between biblical wisdom and knowledge.

Wisdom is the result of using the knowledge that you have gained. Knowledge, for the sake of knowledge, doesn't mean a thing. The Bible clearly states that knowledge puffs one up with pride, and when pride comes, so does shame (1 Corinthians 8:1, Proverbs 11:2).

My example is a depiction of the fruit obtained from the "tree of the knowledge" which exists today. Many believe that simply because they have completed the requirements to earn a degree (gained knowledge), that they are wise. They haven't used their knowledge yet to prove their wisdom. Because of the financial constraint they have imposed upon themselves, countless will not be able to use their knowledge in the field they have chosen, simply because they must pay the cost of obtaining knowledge without wisdom. As this happens, many experience the shame of having gained knowledge but not being able to exercise it as they had anticipated.

The kingdom is not some affair that just gets brought out on Sundays; it applies to all areas of our lives. I could have chosen any of a number of other "worldly" topics to explore, such as the shame points found in the criminal justice system in this country, the shame points on fathers dealing with child support matters, or the shame points on drug abuse in elderly care.

Or would it have been better to focus on the shame points found in the divorce rate in church which exceeds the rate of those unchurched couples; the controlling and domineering spirit on pastors from the Lord's flock; the increasing number of church leaders addicted to pornography; the high turnover of pastors leaving the church for secular work, due to burn-out from their congregation; the number of pastor's kids leaving the ministry because of the duplicity they have witnessed in their lives; or a church that is frightened to take on social issues for fear of losing members and the financial hit that such actions would bring? Shame is no respecter of person; it is an equal opportunity punisher. Each of these conditions and host of others need to have the one and only answer from the Kingdom of Grace.

Part 3
The Solution

Shame is destroyed by authenticity and love.
Shame is anything which tries to cover-up how God sees you to
be.   The first Adam covered himself up, but the last Adam
showed his nakedness to show how we have covered ourselves.

3.1 Full of Grace

*(14) And the Word was made flesh, and dwelt among us, (and we beheld his glory, the glory as of the only begotten of the Father,) **full of grace and truth**. (15) John bare witness of him, and cried, saying, "This was he of whom I spake. He that cometh after me is preferred before me: for he was before me. (16) And of his fullness have all we received, and **grace for grace**. (17) For the law was given by Moses, but **grace and truth came by Jesus Christ**." – John 1:14-17*

The book of John is unique in the Greek language. This passage contains the only mention of grace (*charis* in the Greek) throughout the entire text. This in itself is interesting, but it is the name of the author which makes this book such a great study on the nature of grace. John is the Anglican name for the person known in Hebrew as "Yochanan," a name that is translated as, "God is gracious." So here you have a book which describes the life of Jesus from the perspective of God's graciousness!

Notice in verse 14 that Jesus as the only begotten of the Father is born into the earth full of grace and truth. There is a point here which many miss when they read the text, so I'm going to draw it out here for a moment, because it is vital in understanding how grace got back into the earth.

If you'll recall in the fall of man back in the garden, grace was disconnected from the realm of heaven by the transgression of the woman and Adam. From this point forward until Jesus, there was not an accurate depiction of the Kingdom of Grace daily operating in the earth through a human. I realize some will take exception to this statement, citing that Noah, Abraham, David, or even the prophets operated from this realm. Yes, this is true, but it was in a measure, not the fullness like Jesus did. So what is my point here? Simply this: How did Jesus, full of grace, come to the earth if the earth hadn't seen any humans walking in the nature of grace since the fall of man?

Jesus, part God, has the grace component from the Kingdom of Heaven. But Jesus, the man, could forever be recognized as disconnected from grace in an earth suit if He didn't share in the grace nature intended for mankind from the beginning. Simply put: At conception, children share in the DNA structure of BOTH parents. This is a structure that I submit to you which spans not only the physical realm but also the spiritual realm. Consider that Jesus in John 8 rebukes the religious leaders by saying they are of their father, the devil. The devil is a spiritual being, not an earthly being. So Jesus' DNA had to take on the properties of both worlds in order for him to be designated "full of grace." So how did it happen?

*(26) And in the sixth month the angel Gabriel was sent from God unto a city of Galilee, named Nazareth, (27) To a virgin espoused to a man whose name was Joseph, of the house of David; and the virgin's name was Mary. (28) And the angel came in unto her, and said, Hail, thou that art **highly favoured, the Lord is with thee: blessed art thou among women.** (29) And when she saw him, **she was troubled at his saying, and cast in her mind what manner of salutation this should be.**
– Luke 1:26-29*

For generations, Hebrew girls had been waiting with eager anticipation for the fulfillment of the prophetic word that said a virgin would birth the Messiah of Israel. In this passage, we see the valiant messenger angel Gabriel came to Mary to make a proclamation from the Kingdom of God. Mary's name has an important meaning in this discussion. It, like the name of John, is the Anglican rendition for the Hebrew name Miriam, which in the Hebrew culture is a very common name, since it represents the sister of Moses and Aaron. Yet it is the meaning of Miriam which is vital to this story, since in Hebrew, it means "rebellious." God is about to conceive His son in rebellion! But this can't happen if grace is to be in operation at the conception.

Before looking at Gabriel's proclamation, let me draw your attention to verse 29 and Mary's reaction to it. Notice how she was troubled by it and wondered what it meant. Obviously, whatever he said in verse 28 can't be as unassuming as it seems to our eyes if it caused that kind of reaction in a person. I mean how often have you said to someone, "you are blessed among women," or, "the Lord is with you," and the person looked at you kind of funny and went, "Huh?" So what gives?

Gabriel's proclamation released a level of grace into the atmosphere which until the fall had never been experienced on earth. The Greek word "charitoō" is what he used in his salutation to Mary, and it means to be highly favored. Yet this meaning pales in comparison to the fullness it delivers. In this word, the entire Kingdom of Grace was granted and imparted to Mary, voiding out all disgrace which resulted from the fall of man. This charge straight from the Throne of Grace opened up the channel for heaven to once again connect with the earthly realm in a symbiotic relationship.

Notice the effect that occurs from this declaration of being highly favored. First, the "Lord is with you." This does not imply that the Lord wasn't with Mary prior to this moment, but from this point forward she would have direct access to the Lord in a manner she had never experienced. In many ways, the access which was granted to her was better than the access that the high priest had in the Holy of Holies since they could only approach the Lord once a year through a series of ceremonial rituals. The access that Esther had to the King is similar to what Mary would experience, and even this falls short of the nature of the meaning of having the Lord with you.

If you want to relate this experience to a standard that we can recognize today, it would be like saying that Mary was the first "saved" person under the new covenant. Before you go and get all bent out of shape with this depiction, realize Mary still had to accept that Jesus was her Lord and go through all the experiences which lead to the new creation reality in a believer. My point is that the relationship which Mary began to experience with the Lord at this point in her life would be in many ways similar to what we experience today in our relationship with Him, but she was operating under the parameters of the old covenant.

The second effect of Gabriel's proclamation is that Mary was "blessed among women." Blessing is a direct result of being in the presence of God. You are not able to escape it. (Why you would want to is beyond me!) This is the result of operating in the Kingdom of Grace which many clamor for but fall short of. Striving for blessings are not what we are supposed to focus our eyes upon but upon the kingdom of God and His righteousness (Matthew 6:33). This means that as you pay attention to the Lord and His presence in your life, the blessing from His kingdom will naturally fall upon you as a result of His grace-giving nature.

I can't stress the importance of this act of Gabriel's enough. As a matter of fact, this word "charitoō", comes from the root word "charis", which you should by now recognize as the term "grace," only occurs two times in the entire New Testament writings—this being the first occurrence and the second being found in Ephesians 1:6:

> To the praise of the glory of his grace, wherein **he hath made us accepted** in the beloved.

In this verse, Paul declares our relationship with the Father has been established in the exact same manner that Mary's relationship with the Lord was. Notice it is according to the glory of His grace that we have been declared "highly favored" or made accepted. It is in this nature of "**charitoō**" which Mary was now able to be a vessel who would permit Jesus to be conceived as the full representation of mankind, as God had originally intended. It is from this position of grace that the fullness John speaks of is given in "grace for grace."

3.2 Understanding the Prodigal

When I began studying the subject of grace, the very first passage that I recall being drawn to was the story of the prodigal son found in Luke 15. Over and over again, this passage would keep coming back to me as I delved deeper into the world of God's grace. Most people know this story is descriptive of how a proud child left the shelter of his father's house, went into the world to make his way but wasted all that he had. Then, he decided to return to his father's house, submitting himself to position of a slave. The response of the father to the return of his son has become the model to all of us of what grace looks like.

I didn't think there was much more which could be mined from this story about the nature of grace, until I began understanding the complexities of shame. I want to open up this passage to you once again, as I discovered it from a teaching I heard recently. I believe that you will finally understand the fullness of what the Father has done for us to overcome the shame which has plagued us.

The Context

Most who teach this story forget to give the context in which it was delivered. This story is actually the third story in Luke 15 where Jesus teaches about the power of kingdom restoration.

(1) Now all the tax collectors and sinners were coming near to listen to him. (2) And the Pharisees and the scribes were grumbling and saying, "This fellow welcomes sinners and eats with them." – Luke 15:1-2

Notice who is in attendance in these stories: tax collectors, sinners, Pharisees and scribes. This list describes pretty much every category of person that the kingdom affects. Tax collectors are those who are bound to a different kingdom which extracts worth in order to prop itself up. Sinners, obviously, are those who are not adhering to the path which God has desired for them to follow. Pharisees are the religious believers who have established their own path to moral rectitude and promote it towards anyone who will fall under its controlling influence, and the scribes are those who adhere to the legal written authority from of a previous revelation, forcing all interactions to be aligned within the scope of these letters.

Each of these classes of people has their own frame of reference, or paradigm, operating when you speak to them about any matter. Each of these parables is designed to cut through their paradigms in order to properly explain about how the Kingdom of God truly functions. I mention this for one reason: Your paradigm— the way that you think—doesn't even come close to how these people thought. So in order for you to properly understand the magnitude of these parables, you need to at least put yourself into the shoes of these people.

Relating the Kingdom to Life

Each parable raises the bar, so to speak, on how the kingdom operates. The first story deals with the matter of a lost sheep. Notice how Jesus begins this parable:

(4) What man of you, having a hundred sheep, if he lose one of them, doth not leave the ninety and nine in the wilderness, and go after that which is lost, until he find it? – Luke 15:4

"What man of you..." brings a natural, every day response out of the men. Jesus is relating to events in their lives that they all can understand, since most, if not all, had dealt with livestock at one time or another in their lives. The desire to find a lost sheep demonstrated the nature of a good husband as defined within their social circle. It is quite possible one of the men there may have just had to perform such a task that very day. Not to go looking for the sheep would be deemed as being an unjust steward of the property you were responsible for. It could be viewed as a disgrace in the eyes of a neighbor who might have to consider whether you are worthy enough to care for their flocks should the matter arise in the future.

Either what woman having ten pieces of silver, if she lose one piece, doth not light a candle, and sweep the house, and seek diligently till she find it? – Luke 15:8

"Either what woman..." addresses the woman in the crowd with a social norm who all would be able to quickly identify with. Many of us unfortunately today don't understand what Jesus is making reference to in this parable. In those days, it was a custom for a woman to receive 10 pieces of silver from her husband upon their engagement. Most often, these pieces were assembled in a headdress which the bride would wear in public signifying that she was betrothed. One of the two most embarrassing things she could experience was being seen in public without the ten pieces of silver, or having one or more of the pieces missing, which signified she had transacted some matter which required her to "sell" her husband's defined worth. This woman would scour the entire house in search of the lost item rather than risk the exposure of public humiliation of not only herself but her husband.

In each of these two parables, Jesus establishes the common theme of joy in the success of the person achieving their reward for recovering that which was lost. Joy, as you'll recall, is the root word of grace. As a wrap up to each story, Jesus relates that the joy which is experienced on the earthly plane has a corresponding representation in the grace-realm of Heaven. Yet, something is about to happen which these people are not prepared for: a redefining of social order according to the Kingdom of God through the example of the prodigal. Permit me to explain.

In the story of the prodigal son, Jesus depicts the most callous condition of all human interaction: the lack of respect for a parent. In this parable, the second son's demand for his inheritance clearly states, "I wish you were dead!" in the ears of all those present. "Shame on him!" is the underlying emotion churning in the hearts of all those listening.

To add to this sense of communal shame, Jesus next states that the son leaves the shelter of the father's domain to squander all of his inheritance in the world through riotous living. Next, he adds to the shame of this young man by attaching him in employment to a "heathen" with the responsibility of tending pigs! Thrust into the heart of a famine, the young man must decide whether to continue working for his employer so he can earn his meal or eat the pods which he fed the pigs with. Coming to his senses, he realizes what he has done and that he could return to his father's house in the position of a slave and be taken care of much better than his present state.

At this point in the story, Jesus played to the social shame which each person could identify with. They all knew what was about to happen to the young man upon his return to his father's house.

> SHAME IS A METRIC OF SOCIAL ORDER THAT VALUES THE TREE OF THE KNOWLEDGE OF GOOD AND EVIL. THE FATHER IS FAR ABOVE SUCH MEASUREMENTS.

Unfortunately, today, we do not share the cultural conscience these people had in the day of this story, and this means that we miss the most significant part of the message. This part, which Jesus is about to relate to them will forever change their understanding of what the Father is doing.

There existed a long regarded custom in the region that when a person ever went away, lost all of their resources and then returned back to the family, their only means of recognition would be that of a slave. The person would be brought into the center of the community, where all would surround the person. A large ceramic pot, which represented the resources which the individual had left the community with, would be placed before the person. During this ceremony, the person's mother would be the only family member permitted to come to the side of the person as a support.

The leaders in the community would come before the returning member and strike the pot intending to smash it to bits as a symbolic gesture of the wasteful conduct that this person had committed. Once they were finished, the entire community would forever recognize this person as someone who had disgraced their family and that they were to be regarded as no better than a slave for the remainder of their days.

This was the common understanding which every person listening to Jesus tell this story was drawing from. So you can sense their resolve to see that the youngest son be dealt with the proper treatment due to one who has squandered the family inheritance. His actions were shameful, and he needs to be made an example of! Jesus even pulled on the social norms in the thoughts of the young man as he declares that he will tell his father he has sinned against Heaven and is only worthy of being a slave—never a son.

> *And he arose, and came to his father. But when he was yet a great way off, his father saw him, and had compassion, and ran, and fell on his neck, and kissed him. – Luke 15:20*

As this words came from the lips of Jesus, I can image that jaws dropped and eyes popped wide open in complete shock to what they were hearing. The prodigal son's story is not about the sons; it is about the father and his compassion. Notice how the father is looking for the son to return. He doesn't know when he will return, so he must have been continually scanning the horizon, waiting for the first indication that his son is approaching.

The compassion of the father is what causes him to run to his son, and he has to run if he is to save his son from the public humiliation and shame which will naturally befall him in his present state. Remember that the mother was the only family member who would be permitted to come to the side of the young man if he came into the community. Fathers traditionally kept themselves away from this public display of shame. The father's love for his son would not permit this to happen. Running to meet his son out away from the community, he embraces him and kisses him. Whatever clung to the pig tender's clothing and skin was now a part of the father in the embrace that he offered. Even as the son is reciting his claims against the father, the father is anxiously trying to restore the son to his rightful position before anyone in the community knows that the son has returned.

A robe and a ring defined the heritage of the house he came from, tokens which clearly displayed a level of honor to the bearer. But it was the call for shoes which elevated the servant in the pig pen to the status of a true son in the house. Each of these items the father recognized as a foil to any shame which any member of the community might try to place upon the son. And it would be a nameless servant who would place these articles upon the lad ushering in the restoration of a family.

This is the story of the father who took all the shame due his son upon himself before anyone else could put it upon the son. We see this in his embrace of his son who had become someone socially unacceptable through the work which he conducted daily. We see it in his running to his son outside the community in order to keep him from the sentence that awaited him therein. We see it in the call for the emblems which signified a son in his house: a robe, a ring and shoes. It almost appears that the father had prepared himself ahead of time for such actions, whenever his son would return.

The full depth of meaning to this story can't permit the response of the oldest son to be forgotten. Understand that the Hebrew culture had a rich tradition for the rights of the first born who would receive a double portion of the inheritance of the estate when the father died. All other heirs would divide the remaining estate equally between them. Even though the father had divided the estate for the youngest son, the oldest son still had his inheritance intact. Yet his unwillingness to accept the radical response which his father has made to his brother becomes a stumbling block to him.

> THE STORY OF THE PRODIGAL IS NOT ABOUT EITHER OF THE SONS. IT IS A STORY ABOUT THE FATHER WHO TOOK ON ALL SHAME BEFORE THE COMMUNITY HAD THE OPPORTUNITY TO PLACE IT UPON THE WAYWARD SON. IT IS ABOUT WHAT THE FATHER DID FOR US.

(29) And he answering said to his father, "Lo, these many years do I serve thee, neither transgressed I at any time thy commandment: and yet thou never gavest me a kid, that I might make merry with my friends: (30) But as soon as this thy son was come, which hath devoured thy living with harlots, thou hast killed for him the fatted calf." – Luke 15:29-30

Notice how this son believes that hard work and strictly following the commandments of the father make for a relationship worthy of celebrating with friends. He perceives that the riotous living his younger brother conducted was approved by the father in the celebration he heard going on. His anger at his brother's past actions keeps him from experiencing the joy of a family experience which will have great rewards for generations to come. This is the

Grace for Shame

shame of the oldest son: allowing bitter emotions to hinder natural relationships.

I want you to consider a couple of things in this entire passage from Luke 15. Recall that the audience who Jesus is speaking to is comprised of four groups of people: the tax collectors and sinners, which are represented in the youngest son, and the Pharisees and scribes, which are represented in the oldest son. Jesus has addressed each of their relationships with the Father in the story of the prodigal by drawing them in with real life examples in the story of the lost sheep and lost coin. This story of the prodigal, unlike the example of the lost sheep and lost coin, makes no direct connecting reference to the Kingdom of God, I believe, to intentionally show that the relationship we have with the Father is not to be compartmentalized for a set period of time, like the Pharisees and scribes would prescribe.

The father demonstrated with the youngest son that their relationship will forever be bound together. Anytime the community sees the youngest son and tries to place the shame of his actions upon him, they will have to recognize the father's actions of restoring the son's rightful position through embracing the shame which was never intended for him.

Finally, in this one story, Jesus demonstrates the fact that everyone in the eyes of the Father is a member of His family. The Pharisees complaint at the opening of Luke 15 was that Jesus was talking and eating with sinners. Their attitude was the same as the older brother towards the father. Jesus' mission was to draw all men to the Father, and in the story of the prodigal, we see the intense love which the Father has for His children and what extreme measures He will take to bring those who have lost their way back to Him.

Consider the shame which Jesus confronted on the cross occurred outside the community of Jerusalem. Once all things had been fulfilled according to the Scriptures, He was embraced by the Father as the Son, cloaked in a robe of righteousness and seated next to the right hand of the Father. Once again, the prodigal story is not about the sons but about the love of the Father towards His sons: you and I!

3.3 Grace Exchange

All that Jesus did on this earth was to correct the results from the fall in the garden. He came to exchange what Adam did so we could have the Kingdom of Grace operating daily in our lives.

And of his fullness have all we received, and grace for grace.
– John 1:16

In this verse, we see what Jesus did was exchange the grace of the kingdom for the grace which operates in the world. But the question is this: Where does this exchange occur? Actually, there are a number of occurrences of exchanges occurring in the life of Jesus, but today, I'm only going to focus on the last one, which was the exchange that reversed the effect of the fall and prepared a place for us to receive the kingdom.

Since the fall of man, there had been a sense of shame surrounding everything man had attempted to accomplish throughout history until Jesus came on the scene to exchange this shame for the honor which comes with living in the kingdom.

We see this in the following verse:

*Looking unto Jesus the author and finisher of our faith; who for the joy that was set before him **endured the cross**, **despising the shame**, and is set down at the right hand of the throne of God.*
– Hebrews 12:2

Notice that while Jesus endured the entire process of the cross, He was at the same time despising the shame which it brought. In the Greek, the word "despising" means to condemn, despise, disdain, and think little or nothing of. What is important in understanding this is that when anyone was crucified by the Romans, it was customary to impale the person to the cross totally naked. The time it took to die on the cross was always witnessed totally naked, not wrapped in some cloth like you see in every picture or statue depicting the crucifixion, with wrapping placed there so we wouldn't feel shame! Look, Jesus is trying to eliminate the cause of shame, so why not let it show like it really did!

The Exchange

In this exchange, there are a number of items which occur in rapid succession in order to correct the first item in the fall as well as prepare a place for us in the kingdom. But before I get into this, I want to bring something out. Throughout the Bible, the Messiah is known as the Son of David. We know David held a special place in God's heart, even to the point of having the eternal Son of God be born through his lineage. This is the highest honor that any one person could possibly achieve, ever. Yet as a king, he suffered the ultimate shame for the lack of discretion which he displayed with Bathsheba and her husband, Uriah. David's repentance for his actions is recorded in Psalms 51, and we'll see in few moments how this song prophetically illustrates the last actions of Jesus on the cross. But I want you to first look at another Psalm from David which strangely portrays the last moments Jesus experienced on the cross.

*(16) Hear me, O LORD; for thy lovingkindness is good: turn unto me according to the multitude of thy tender mercies. (17) And hide not thy face from thy servant; for I am in trouble: hear me speedily. (18) Draw nigh unto my soul, and redeem it: deliver me because of mine enemies. (19) Thou hast known my **reproach, and my shame, and my dishonour**: mine adversaries are all before thee. (20) **Reproach** hath broken my heart; and I am full of heaviness: and I looked for some to take pity, but there was none; and for comforters, but I found none. (21) They gave me also gall for my meat; and in my thirst they gave me vinegar to drink. – Psalms 69:16-21*

Notice how David is dealing with shame and dishonor in this passage. Yet also notice that the term reproach is also mentioned. The standard definition for this term means "that which causes shame or disgrace," yet in the Hebrew, this word means to disgrace by pulling off and exposing the nakedness of someone. Keep this in mind as we move towards Jesus' last moments on the cross. In the following passage from John 19 we will find what we need to be aware of how this exchange transpired and see the lines of Psalm 69 played out.

*(25) Now there stood by the cross of Jesus his mother, and his mother's sister, Mary the wife of Cleophas, and Mary Magdalene. (26) When Jesus therefore saw his mother, and the disciple standing by, whom he loved, he saith unto his mother, **"Woman, behold thy son!"** (27) Then saith he to the disciple, **"Behold thy mother!"** And from that hour that disciple took her unto his own home. (28) After this, Jesus **knowing that all things were now accomplished**, that the Scripture might be fulfilled, saith, "I thirst." (29) Now there was set a vessel full of vinegar: and they filled **a sponge with vinegar, and put it upon hyssop, and put it to his mouth. (30)** When Jesus therefore had received the vinegar, he said, It is finished: and he bowed his head, and gave up the ghost. – John 19:25-30*

Notice first in verse 25 Jesus, naked upon the cross and bearing the sins of all mankind, is viewed by three women each with the name of Mary. The name "Mary," as I've stated previously, is the Hebrew word "Miriam," which means rebellion. One of those women is his mother, the very woman that God declared to be "highly favored"—a *charis* word, which means she was returned to the original intent of God that the woman held in the garden prior to the fall.

The second Mary is His aunt. Notice how rebellion runs in the family! Fortunately, there is the uncle to change all of this. Cleophas is a unique name simply because, in Hebrew and well as in the Greek, it means the same thing: exchange. In this drama, the Father strategically placed an exchange to witness the exchange! Brilliant!

The third, Mary Magdalene, is an important person in these final hours of the ministry of Jesus. You should pay attention to every person who is listed in the Bible with two names. Magdalene means tower. It comes from a root word which means to twist, be large; in sense of body, mind, estate, honor, pride—to boast, increase, magnify, promote. Think of the tower of Babel, and you get the picture: man's biggest rebellion after the flood. Jesus is surrounded by rebellion, and He is about to make the exchange of a lifetime.

In verse 26, we find there is another person present at the cross with the women. In Hebrew, John's name means "God is gracious." Notice how Jesus addresses His mother: "Woman." In this matter, He is clearly indicating she represents the woman from the garden—a woman full of the grace of the Kingdom of God. At this moment, He was calling her to look upon the disgrace which He is enveloped in. Yet even the other women must have looked at the figure before them, since it is probable they did not know whom Jesus was speaking to.

Recall that Jesus, prior to these events, walked in the fullest measure of grace from the kingdom. However now having been separated from the Father by the sins of mankind which had been placed upon Him, He is exchanging His kingdom grace for all the world's sins since the fall.

In verse 27, we see the completion of the exchange in His comment to John. What is said there is much more than "Behold your mother!" What really is being said there is this: "You, who is known as God is gracious, look at the woman who is the fullest measure of the grace from the kingdom, because she is what I've always intended for mankind. Your name now reflects your lineage."

In verse 28, we can see Jesus is still fully aware of the fact that there is an agenda which He is fulfilling. So now all He has to do is make preparations for us to receive the Holy Spirit. Before I explain this, let me bring into this a passage from Psalms 51.

*(5) Behold, I was shapen in iniquity; and in sin did my mother conceive me. (6) Behold, thou desirest **truth in the inward parts**: and in the hidden part thou shalt make me to know wisdom. (7) **Purge me with hyssop**, and I shall be clean: wash me, and I shall be whiter than snow. (8) Make me to hear joy and gladness; that the bones which thou hast broken may rejoice. (9) Hide thy face from my sins, and blot out all mine iniquities. – Psalms 51:5-9*

As I stated previously, this song is the response that David made to his greatest disgrace as a king. Notice in verse 5 we see his declaration of his birth. Jesus had to live with this same declaration from those who knew of his apparent "natural" conception.

In verse 6, we see mention of truth in the inward parts. This is a prophetic reference to the Holy Spirit living inside us, as Jesus would declare in John 14:17, *"Even the Spirit of truth; whom the world cannot receive, because it seeth him not, neither knoweth him: but ye know him; for he dwelleth with you, and shall be in you."*

But there is a slight problem. If the Holy Spirit is to reside inside of us through Jesus, and He is presently upon the cross, the Holy Spirit will not be able to come close to Him, since He is "defiled" by sin.

Look at verse 7 in Psalms 51 and verse 29 from John 19. Can you see the one thing which is similar in both? I trust you were able to see that hyssop was mentioned in each verse. What does this mean? Hyssop is the key ingredient which the priests used to clean and purify those items or people who had become defiled—a term meaning that we're no longer able to come into the presence of God.

Today, we have lost the medicinal importance of this ingredient, yet according to scientific studies it has a number of benefits.

Hyssop, also known as origanum vulgare, is a wild, mountain-grown oregano found exclusively in the Mediterranean. Origanum vulgare contains 49 phytoelements with medicine-like results in preventing and reversing illness and disease within nine areas of the body (Phytochemical and Ethnobotanical databases-AGR).

Origanum vulgare contains 41 antibacterial elements, 31 anti-inflammatory elements, 26 antiviral elements, 26 antifungal elements and 6 antiparasitic elements effective against MRSA, Pseudomonas, Staphylococcus, colds, influenza, athlete's foot, Candida and internal parasites. It includes 22 antiseptic elements that provide relief for bites, abrasions and sore throats. In addition, it contains 28 antioxidant and 6 immunostimulant elements, which are important in preventing disease, and 4 COX-2 inhibitor elements, which have an anti-inflammatory effect for brain function.[3]

It is my belief here in John 19, had Jesus stated that "it is finished" before having the hyssop come to His mouth, we would not have had a "clean" vessel for Holy Spirit to reside in. But because Jesus took the vinegar into His mouth by way of the hyssop, it purged and cleansed His inward parts so truth could reside there. (As I stated, this is purely my belief. However this action was important enough for the Holy Spirit to record, so it has some significance which may still need to be revealed to us.)

Now in verse 8, we find something which makes our opening verse from Hebrews 12 more meaningful. The latter part of the verse mentions there were bones that were broken. We know there were no bones broken in the body of Jesus, so how is this verse speaking of the same thing? The word "bones" in verse 8 also means body. We know that Jesus' body was clearly broken according to Isaiah 53, so this lets us know that the joy which Jesus

---

[3] www.hysophealth.com/pages/home.php

endured on the cross came from a body which was broken in exchange for us.

3.4 Why the Cross – Part 1

Ask a believer why Jesus died, and you will probably hear this: "To redeem me from my sin," or "To save me from my sins." These answers are correct in explaining the substitution which Jesus made on our behalf, but let me ask you this question: Why did He die on a cross?

I want you to think for a moment. During the days when Jesus walked upon the face of the earth, how many ways could a person be killed? I ask this because if Jesus just died for our sins, couldn't His death have been accomplished in some other manner? His cousin John was beheaded; a sword would have completed the task swiftly; even the centurion who pierced the side of Jesus as He hung on the cross understood that a spear into the heart would have accomplished the same result in an expedient fashion. So why the cross?

The cross as we know it was first employed by Alexander the Great. As he made his conquest of the known world, the cross was used as a means of imposing capital punishment. One such instance of Alexander's use of this device came after a particular battle, when one of Alexander's favorite generals lie mortally wounded in Alexander's presence. The doctor, being commanded to quickly respond to the general's wounds, was unable to keep the general from dying. Furious with the doctor, Alexander had him and all of the attending staff crucified as retribution.

Crucifixion was not intended to be an instantaneous death instrument. Its purpose was to cause the person being suspended to endure agonizing pain and suffering over many days, if not weeks, in front of multitudes of people. The cross was either in the shape of an "x" or the "t" which is most commonly known. The "t" device was comprised of two separate parts: the vertical unit, which was often planted into the ground wherever the execution was to take place, often outside of the town; and the horizontal beam, which weighing somewhere around 150 pounds or more, was strapped to the convicted person's arms. It was then required that it be carried from the place of judgment to the place of execution. Once the convicted person arrived at the execution place, he would be hoisted up onto the vertical element, still attached to the horizontal beam. A small platform would be attached to the vertical element, which would be the only support for the body. Once positioned on the cross, the victim would reside until he starved to death, or unable to support himself anymore, the weight of his slumping body caused him to asphyxiate.

The duration of a crucifixion was intentional since it permitted the population to witness the effect on the convicted soul over a long, drawn out period of time and act as a warning towards anyone who would attempt to perpetrate similar actions. Even in the crucifixion of Jesus, this was intentional and can be seen in these verses.

(43) Joseph of Arimathaea, an honourable counsellor, which
also waited for the kingdom of God, came, and went in boldly

unto Pilate, and craved the body of Jesus. (44) And Pilate
marvelled if he were already dead: and calling unto him the
centurion, he asked him whether he had been any while dead.
(45) And when he knew it of the centurion, he gave the body to
Joseph. – Mark 15:43-45

Notice in verse 44 that Pilate marveled, or was surprised Jesus had already died. Only six hours had passed since He was suspended on the cross. He knew that crucifixion didn't kill someone in such a short period of time. This is why he called the centurion to confirm what Joseph had claimed. You can be assured the centurion would not lie to a royal governor about a matter such as this.

Okay, so now you know a little more about the purpose of crucifixion. It was a tool of the state which was intended to be long and agonizing, and it was to be done in full view of the public as a warning to others who might have entertained similar thoughts and aspirations that the convicted was charged with. I also recognize that you may have already known much of this, so why bring it out into the open? Simply because my question to you still remains inadequately answered: Why the cross? I claimed I would make you think about this, and I trust that you have been. But do you have any answer beyond the material which I've already covered? If not, let this be an aid to you.

Looking unto Jesus the author and finisher of our faith; who for
the joy that was set before him endured the cross, despising the
shame, and is set down at the right hand of the throne of God.
– Hebrews 12:2

Jesus, knowing the joy which was to come in this world and in Heaven, endured all the physical agony of being nailed to the cross.

His joints being disconnected, and the pain of the vertical beam pressing against the lacerations that had been ripped into His back. He endured the emotional agony of the cross which He was suspended upon even as He cried out to God, "Why have you forsaken me!" Knowing that the sins of the world were being placed upon Him in those hours of darkness, becoming accursed of God, simply because He was charged for admitting the truth that He was the Son of God, just like the first Adam was before Him.

Yet while Jesus endured all of this, He was actively doing something else; something so very important to the mission of Him being the Author and Finisher of your faith that without Him doing this very act, all of our faith would be useless towards the onslaught of the enemy's schemes and devices. Do you know what He was doing? This verse tells us He was despising the shame while on the cross. What shame?

There are so many levels of shame in this event which you could park here for years and study them and their implications. But let me deal with just one for now, one which is the primary, most glaring one. When I ask people to describe what the crucifixion of Jesus looks like, the responses I get are all pretty similar: Jesus nailed to a cross; arms outstretched; a crown of thrones on His head; a thin loincloth stained from the blood of the lashings which He took; and His beard and hair are matted from the blood dripping off of His body.

While this might be horrific to envision in its full splendor, many don't recognize what could be the element of shame that Jesus is despising. Permit me to make a slight clarification to the accuracy of the description made above. Jesus did not wear a loincloth or any clothing for that matter. He was naked. He hung on a cross completely naked, stripped of any garment that might hide His genitals. Yes, He was intentionally, willfully and shamefully exposed for six hours to all who passed by or stopped to look upon the scene, which included the women who had followed him during His 3 ½ year ministry. Naked as the day when He was born was the condition He was in when He died.

Let me ask you this question: How would you feel if you had to hang for six hours between Heaven and Earth, fully exposed to both worlds, proclaimed guilty through a deceptive act? Embarrassed, humiliated, even shameful? Realize at that moment, He was on the cross representing you and me. So don't tell me you don't know what shame He despised on the cross.

Let me reiterate the purpose of the cross: It was a device for capital punishment designed first to inflict shame as a means of controlling the actions of others planning to take similar actions against the state; its ultimate result leading to death. In His days on this earth, Jesus understood this, as did every person in the Roman Empire. Let's look at the actions of those who witnessed the scene at the crucifixion of Jesus.

> *(25) And it was the third hour, and they crucified him. (26) And the superscription of his accusation was written over, THE KING OF THE JEWS. (27) And with him they crucify two thieves; the one on his right hand, and the other on his left. (28) And the scripture was fulfilled, which saith, And he was numbered with the transgressors. (29) And they that passed by railed on him, wagging their heads, and saying, Ah, thou that destroyest the temple, and buildest it in three days, (30) Save thyself, and come down from the cross. (31) Likewise also the chief priests mocking said among themselves with the scribes, He saved*

others; himself he cannot save. (32) Let Christ the King of Israel descend now from the cross, that we may see and believe. And they that were crucified with him reviled him. – Mark 15:25-32

Notice the insulting tone of shame which is being hurled at Jesus by those passing by, the priests who witnessed this event, and even the others convicted with Him. This is the intention of the cross in its achievement – shame, embarrassment, and humiliation from all the governing forces (i.e. political, religious, spiritual) in the region.

This is the biggest exchange which grace can give to you, but you need to see this exchange as it was viewed from the Kingdom of Grace.

3.5 The Extent of Shame

In the book of "God is gracious," more commonly known as John, most Bible scholars will tell you there are what is known as the seven "I am" statements of Jesus. Each of these statements provides to us an identity of the nature and persona of Jesus, not only during His earthly lifetime but also His eternal lifetime. To refresh your memory what these statements are, I have listed them below for you.

1. **The Bread of Life**
    (John 6:51) I am the living bread which came down from heaven. If anyone eats of this bread, he will live forever; and the bread that I shall give is My flesh, which I shall give for the life of the world."

2. **Light of the World**
    (John 8:12) Then Jesus spoke to them again, saying, "I am the light of the world. He who follows Me shall not walk in darkness, but have the light of life."

3. **The Door**
    (John 10:9) I am the door. If anyone enters by Me, he will be saved, and will go in and out and find pasture. "

4. **The Good Shepherd**
    (John 10:11) "I am the good shepherd. The good shepherd gives His life for the sheep."

5. **The Resurrection and Life**
    (John 11:25) Jesus said to her, "I am the resurrection and the life. He who believes in Me, though he may die, he shall live."

6. **The Way, the Truth and the Life**

   (John 14:6) *Jesus said to him, "I am the way, the truth, and the life. No one comes to the Father except through Me."*

7. **The Vine**

   (John 15:5) *"I am the vine, you are the branches. He who abides in Me, and I in him, bears much fruit; for without Me you can do nothing."*

Each of these very familiar statements is to those of us who are saved, and they have even become a banner to our declaration of faith in Jesus. We relate to them based on the earthly ministry of Jesus, simply because we live on earth too. There are three other "I am" statements made by Jesus in the Gospel of John which for some strange reason never get included in this list. They are:

8. **The Teacher and Lord**

   (John 13:13) You call Me Teacher and Lord, and you say well, for so I am.

9. **The Son of God**

   (John 10:36) do you say of Him whom the Father sanctified and sent into the world, 'You are blaspheming,' because I said, 'I am the Son of God'?

10. **The King**

    (John 18:37) Pilate therefore said to Him, "Are You a king then?" Jesus answered, "You say rightly that I am a king. For this cause I was born, and for this cause I have come into the world, that I should bear witness to the truth. Everyone who is of the truth hears My voice."

I'm not going to pick apart the reasons as to why these three statements don't get included in the seven above. It's obvious that we all know these statements define a role of Jesus which many, if not most people, associate with the deity of Jesus. But these are claims that Jesus made as a man on this earth. According to any teaching that you may have heard about the nature of Jesus when He walked upon this earth, His heavenly attributes were voluntarily relinquished so He could properly depict the role of the last Adam. So what is the point of all this?

Let me first reiterate the purpose of the cross: It was a device for capital punishment designed first to inflict shame as a means of controlling the actions of others planning to take similar actions against the state; its ultimate result leading to death. Now I want you to consider this: All of these titles or claims made by Jesus about who He was, the ten represented here, the ones which you've claimed and identified with as an act of faith in your life, all got nailed to the cross with the man! Every single one experienced the massive force of shame. Let me explain how for a couple of them.

I am the Light of the World. The first utterance of God in the creation events in Genesis 1 was, "Let there be light." In the Hebrew thinking, the word, or voice of God is the light which brings life to the world. This claim of Jesus defines him as the Word of God which brings life, a statement that John declared in the opening of his Gospel, *"In the beginning was the Word, and the Word was with God, and the Word was God. . . In him was life; and the life was the light of men."* When Jesus was preaching on the mountainside to the people, He claimed, *"You are the light of the world. A city that is set on a hill cannot be hid. Neither do men light a candle, and put it under a bushel, but on a candlestick; and it gives light unto all that are in the house. Let your light so shine before men, that they may see your good works, and glorify your Father which is in heaven. "*

Jerusalem is a city built on a hill, and Golgotha is a hill where the crucifixion was conducted, since it gave all the surrounding communities ample opportunity to witness the events. Three hours into the crucifixion, during the middle of the day, the skies became dark, or put another way, the light went out. How can Jesus be the light of the world, which gives life? As everyone can see, His life was being taken away. What does it matter that He did good works? His claims put him on the same level as God!

A sidebar here: Seventy years from this time, in Rome, the Emperor Nero would regularly crucify thousands of believers. In one such incident, he conducted an evening crucifixion of hundreds of men, women and children in the gardens surrounding the palace, while he held a royal festival in the palace. The candle light for this festival was supplied by the live burning bodies of those suspended between heaven and earth in honor of their Lord.

I am the Way, the Truth and the Life. Everyone knows that the only way to the Father was through the ceremonial practices of the priesthood defined by Moses. The offering had to be spotless and not bruised, clearly not the image of the man hanging on the cross. How can anyone come to the Father who is being hung on a cross, since this person is cursed anyway? Consider this too: The passage from Isaiah 53, dealing with the suffering servant, which declares that, "By his stripes you are healed," has been clearly associated by a number of Bible scholars with the beating which Jesus took prior to the crucifixion. Your healing, gained by those stripes, now had to endure the shame of the cross.

I am the King. This is the greatest shame ever inflicted upon a dignitary. The act of crucifying someone in the Roman culture was

Grace for Shame

to be reserved for "common" people. Royalty that had been overthrown was paraded through Rome by the conquering general as a means of supreme humiliation. Many would subsequently be exiled to some place in the realm but accommodated with the trappings which still recognized their previous status. To resort to the practice of crucifixion as a punishment on people of such high estate was considered contemptible to the kingdom that had secured the victory. This is why afterwards Pilot agonized over what had been performed on Jesus. As a member of the political class of Rome, he understood the ramifications of his actions if Jesus truly should have been of the royal class. The last thing that he wanted to be responsible for was conflict with a foreign government whose strengths he knew nothing about. He would only proceed with the act once he had secured the agreement of the populous that would be held responsible for all actions taken against this royal subject. But even this agreement vexed his soul for some time afterwards.

In these few examples, we see a depth to the level of shame which many have never considered. Yet I would like to suggest that Jesus knew even greater shame would be associated with his mission on earth. Take a look at this verse from Mark 8.

(34) And when he had called the people unto him with his disciples also, he said unto them, "Whosoever will come after me, let him deny himself, and take up his cross, and follow me. (35) For whosoever will save his life shall lose it; but whosoever shall lose his life for my sake and the gospel's, the same shall save it. (36) For what shall it profit a man, if he shall gain the whole world, and lose his own soul? (37) Or what shall a man give in exchange for his soul? (38) Whosoever therefore shall be ashamed of me and of my words in this adulterous and sinful

generation; of him also shall the Son of man be ashamed, when he cometh in the glory of his Father with the holy angels."
– Mark 8:34-38

This passage has been the standard by which true discipleship has been measured in the life of a believer. Note in verse 38 Jesus clearly attaches the mantel of shame to any person who improperly views His work on the cross, according the standards of the world. Yet, even here, Jesus clearly defines the condition of the society whereby the shame will be attached as a "sinful and adulterous generation." But isn't that every generation?

Each of us must be diligent in following the example Jesus set before us if we are to pick up our cross. This even means understanding what the whole purpose of the cross represented according to the Kingdom of Heaven.

3.6 Why the Cross – Part 2

My question still remains unanswered: Why the cross? Many might consider that the answer may have been answered in the previous chapters, yet I'm still not fully satisfied as it relates to the topic of shame. Fortunately, the full answer is right before us if you're willing to do a little historical research. If you're open to the discovery, consider the following information.

> *Christ hath redeemed us from the curse of the law, being made a curse for us: for it is written, Cursed is every one that hangeth on a tree... – Galatians 3:13*

In this verse, Paul is relating to the Galatians how Christ finished the Law that they were being coerced into by members who had come from Jerusalem. Here he pulls a very well known principle from the Law, which addresses the practice of dealing with the body of a criminal as an explanation to the effect the Law had on people. The original verse he is quoting is found in Deuteronomy 21.

> *And if a man have committed a sin worthy of death, and he be to be put to death, and thou hang him on a tree: (23) His body shall not remain all night upon the tree, but thou shalt in any wise bury him that day; (for he that is hanged is accursed of God;) that thy land be not defiled, which the LORD thy God giveth thee for an inheritance. – Deuteronomy 21:22-23*

The rabbinic teaching of this passage establishes the premise that should a criminal be put to death, his body shall not be hung from a tree overnight since this would defile the land. A dead body was the worst thing which could make someone ceremonially unclean. The concern was that wild animals would somehow attack the carcass of the criminal and scatter it all about the land, hence causing its defilement. Therein lays the stipulation for having the body taken down before nightfall.

Another aspect of this was brought out in a few of the commentaries was that this ordinance was created not because this was the fashion which was sought to deal with criminals, but because this practice was already being performed in the land that the children of Israel were headed into. A common practice in the region was to take the convicted criminal, chop off his head, and place it on a pike or long spear, which was placed at the entrance of the village. The body was also suspended in the air, or from the walls of the community, to act as a warning to all that this was the punishment which one could expect for a transgression. The body and head would be displayed for many days, if not weeks, during which time the birds and animals in the area were given free access to the carcass—a sight which further drove home the point to the community members.

Most of the commentaries state that this type of punishment was meted out primarily to idolaters. Yet because the person was made in the image and likeness of God, there still was a measure of honor due to the person to have their burial quickly to allow the mourning process to begin.

The passage from Deuteronomy comes as Israel is poised to enter the Promised Land after wandering in the wilderness for forty years. Every person between the age of 40 and 60 could possibly recall what it was like to live in Egypt and what it was like to walk through the Red Sea with Pharaoh closely pursuing behind. These same people remember that as children they once had the same opportunity placed before them to enter the land, but the disbelief of their parents kept them out.

Meanwhile, those under 40, along with the older group, had witnessed the manna from heaven, the water from the rock, the presence of God by the fire at night and the cloud by day. They had observed the feasts of Passover, Pentecost, and Tabernacles with Moses and Aaron. While some from the older group might recall the idols of Egypt, this younger group had only seen the idolatry of the nations they had traveled through.

Everyone could recall the incident which happened in Baal-Peor when the women of the land seduced some of the men of Israel, which caused a divinely ordained plague to spread throughout the camp. It wasn't until Phineas took action and killed one of the women and a man from Israel in the tent of the man that the plague stopped.

This ordinance in Deuteronomy is intended to reinforce the relationship that God had with the children of Israel as their only one true God. Since the rabbis have indicated that this regulation was intended for idolaters, you should understand that the tree which is spoken of here is not any ordinary tree.

In the lands that Israel was about to enter into, there were many tribes who practiced various forms of idol worship. The names may have varied for the particular idol being worshipped, but the representations were all very similar: They either were a wooden pole or tree, singular or set in a grove. These poles/trees are most commonly referred to as "Ashtoreth" in the Bible and were the places of worship for the female counterpart of Baal. Both of these gods, Baal and Ashtoreth, were considered fertility gods in the land of Canaan, and many sacrifices were made regularly by the inhabitants in the land so as to guarantee rain, good crops, a plentiful harvest, healthy livestock, fruitful families, and a myriad of others special occasions. Prostitution was a regular occurrence at any of these places as was the slaughter of animals, humans, and even children.

In Hebrew, the meaning of Baal is "possessor" or "husband," while Ashtoreth means "increase of flocks." Within each of these names, we see the subtle nature of how the children would eventually embrace the worship of these very idols which they were forbidden to have any part of. Jehovah was the husband of Israel, having made a covenant with them at Mt. Horeb as they moved toward the Promised Land. As they obeyed the terms of the covenant, the people of Israel would receive the blessing of God's provision in their lives, which included having all of their livestock produce greatly for them. If they transgressed the covenant with God, then they would not see the provision they needed, and their livestock would not reproduce.

Throughout much of the Old Testament writings, we find Israel falling into idol worship, either as a corporate body led by their king or individually. Much of the dealing which God had with Israel once they entered the Promised Land had to do with chastising them for their failings in following Him as their God. Their defeats in battle, their subjection to the kingdoms around them, and even their deportation to Babylon were a direct response to their idol worship. The prophets were constantly warning Israel of their shame and how they would be judged by God for turning their backs on Him.

In the book of Hosea, we see how God feels as He instructed Hosea how he was to live his life in the community of Israel as a prophetic sign of God's judgment on their actions. Hosea, who some claim comes from the priestly order, was required to marry a whore, and despite his love for her, he was not permitted to stop her activities. He fathers three children by her and names each one according to specific transgressions of the people of Israel. This family was a prophetic picture of one thing in Israel: shame!

In God's eyes, all of this idol worship simply cast shame upon the people who He had joined himself to. The book of Jeremiah addresses the shame which Israel was subjected to from all their past idol worshipping. It had led them to being overthrown by a foreign power, having their youngest and brightest taken into Babylon and spread about the kingdom, while their oldest and most feeble were left behind. The worst shame inflicted upon Israel was when the temple of God was desecrated and utterly destroyed by the invading forces.

In returning back to the passage from Deuteronomy, the transgressor who worshipped a false idol depicted as an Ashtoreth would be hung from the very idol they worshipped as a means of desecrating the very object which had been the offense. Subsequently, the pole/tree would be chopped down and burned so there would be no ability for another to commit the same offense with the same object. The community would recognize that the person treated in this manner bore the supreme judgment and shame as an idol worshipper being cursed by Jehovah, who was the one true God. This sheds some light on the passage from Paul in 1 Corinthians 1.

(23) but we preach Christ crucified, to the Jews a stumbling block and to the Greeks foolishness.

The cross was associated with idol worshippers. The Jews refused to acknowledge that their past actions of worshipping other idols could never be completely remitted through the sacrifices of bulls and goats which they offered to Jehovah in repentance. This is why it became, and still is, a stumbling block to them. Recall that the sole reason the High Priest condemned Jesus to the cross was because Jesus claimed, truthfully, to be the son of God. This is a transgression which equaled idolatry in their interpretation of the Scriptures. Such an offense against God was subject to the most severe capital punishment according to their rulings, but they were not able to complete such a task without the approval of the occupying government!

Unable to understand that even their very course of action was a testament of shame to a continued failure to adhere to the covenant they professed to have with God, the governmental-appointed priesthood instructed the temple guards to hand Jesus over to Herod. He then transferred him to Pilate to exact the judgment the priesthood deemed was required by their standards.

At this junction, I want to introduce another idol worshipped in the land: Baal-Hamon, the Lord of the multitude. This particular idol was mentioned once in the Song of Solomon as a place.

> Solomon had a vineyard at Baalhamon; he let out the vineyard unto keepers; every one for the fruit thereof was to bring a thousand pieces of silver. – Song of Solomon 8:11

Many commentators have noted that this particular idol was worshipped for its ability to increase or multiply wealth. This passage demonstrates its connection with an abundance of silver. Yet I want to give further light into the meaning of Hamon. There is within its definition the terms abundance, company, many, multitude, tumult, and rumbling, which leads us into the root meaning of the word hamon, which is to make a loud noise, to be in a great commotion and confusion, to rage, war, tumult, moan and clamor.

My purpose in bringing this aspect to light is so you can see the effect of this type of idol worship on the people dealing with Jesus. Notice that Judas, for thirty pieces of silver, turned Jesus over to the priests. A multitude of temple guards came to secure him in the garden. Unable to find any guilt in Jesus, Pilate addressed the multitude to see if they wanted to exchange prisoners, only to hear the angry words of the mob that Jesus was to be crucified. Here is this exchange recorded in Matthew.

> (24)When Pilate saw that he could prevail nothing, but that rather a tumult was made, he took water, and washed his hands before the multitude, saying, I am innocent of the blood of this just person: see ye to it. (25) Then answered all the people, and said, His blood be on us, and on our children. – Matthew 27:24-25

Can you see all the facets of shame at work here as grace moves into position? A friendship betrayed for the potential of monetary gain; a true son of God being accused of idolatry; our heavenly High Priest being judged by a governmentally appointed priest rather than the priest appointed by God's standards; our King being treated as a idol worshipper; and the consequences of an impassioned decision from an inflamed multitude which will be passed down on their children who just a few days before had welcomed Jesus in Jerusalem as their King.

Do you begin to understand now how Jesus despised the shame as He endured the cross? This is why the cross is the power of the Kingdom of God. This is how grace deals with the matter of shame.

3.7 The Shame of Disappointment

When I described the spiritual definition of shame back in the chapter about the ugly trio, I mentioned that the definition of the Hebrew word for shame contained the aspects of disappointment and confounding. Knowing what you do about the nature of shame, it might seem a bit odd that these two additional definitions would be included in a word describing shame. Yet their descriptive nature is very pertinent to how the Hebrew's associated shame with the worship of idols. I want to take a brief moment to point out these facets here so you can see how the exchange of Jesus addressed these aspects too.

Disappointment is the belief that you have been separated from or missed an appointment. Frequently many associate appointment with time, as in a doctor's appointment. Yet consider that God, who operates in an eternal realm, isn't concerned with time-based appointments. In a kingdom, appointments are a designation to an office; a decree, a direction or command; an allowance; or a grant to a charitable cause. A disappointment in a kingdom means a separation from your assignment and all the means which that assignment requires for it to be fulfilled.

In God's Kingdom, we generate kingdom disappointments based on timely disappointments we have produced. Don't believe that statement? Let me ask you this: Have you ever been halted in your walk because God didn't do something when you expected Him to do it? Welcome to the disappointment of time, or the shame of not working with God.

> Now when the people saw that Moses **delayed** coming down from the mountain, the people gathered together to Aaron, and said to him, "Come, make us gods that shall go before us; for as for this Moses, the man who brought us up out of the land of Egypt, we do not know what has become of him." – Exodus 32:1

In this passage, we see the children of Israel have become disappointed at the delay of Moses on the Mount. The highlighted word "delayed" is the Hebrew word for shame.   Their disappointment with time caused them to shamefully demand Aaron make a god for them. Notice in their communication to Aaron, they distanced themselves from the work of Moses, despite all that had happened through his hand. This is the key to disappointment: break all associations with everyone who caused the delay in order to gain back a perceived loss in our personal control of life.

These people never had a personal revelation of God, and so out of a desperate need for salvation, they attached themselves to someone who knew God, expecting his relationship with God would sustain them. (Hey! That sounds like...) In this act, they elevated a man to the position of "god," and not being able to meet the demand placed upon him to provide for the mass, they became disappointed at their choice of the "provider" and immediately sought to create a different provider who they could worship. This is common in all forms of idol worship. Idols do not have to be crafted images; man is made in the image and likeness of God! Worship of man will always produce disappointment, just as if he had been carved from stone or wood.

When a person places their trust in an inanimate object, there comes a moment of realization of the absurdity in misplaced trust. Confounded why the idol wasn't able to perform the desire sought, disappointment ensues. A limitation has been uncovered that previously had not been expected. For all the joy which comes in promoting an all-encompassing god, the reality of the ratio of unfilled petitions to the religious demands of attentive sacrifice confounds the mind. Paul would call this an "imagination that is exalted above the knowledge of Christ. "

Even in this arena of shame's descriptive nature, we have Jesus making assurance of His purpose on the cross. We find this in the last chapter of the Gospel of Luke in a very familiar story about the disciple's trip down a road towards the town of Emmaus.

> *(13) And, behold, two of them went that same day to a village called Emmaus, which was from Jerusalem about threescore furlongs. (14) And they talked together of all these things which had happened. (15) And it came to pass, that, while they communed together and reasoned, Jesus himself drew near, and went with them. (16) But their eyes were holden that they should not know him. (17) And he said unto them, What manner of communications are these that ye have one to another, as ye walk, and are sad? (18) And the one of them, whose name was Cleopas, answering said unto him, Art thou only a stranger in Jerusalem, and hast not known the things which are come to pass there in these days? (19) And he said unto them, What things? And they said unto him, Concerning Jesus of Nazareth, which was a prophet mighty in deed and word before God and all the people. – Luke 24:13-19*

Notice in verse thirteen as the two disciples walked discussing the events, their reasoning kept them from seeing Jesus. Whenever your thoughts try to justify the results that you never expected, you narrow your field of vision to only see what aligns with your dashed expectations, not what was the solution already at hand.

Next, notice the response in verse 18 and 19 made by the disciple when Jesus asks what they are talking about. In verse 18, Cleophas questions where Jesus has been to miss the events of the last few days. Disappointment will always attempt to bring others into its domain in order to build a stronger sense of loss.

In verse 19, he claims that Jesus was prophet. Just consider that less than a week had passed since the entire city of Jerusalem was hailing that Jesus was the Messiah. The fall from Messiah to prophet is indicative of an appointment missed in the thoughts of the people. The stream of time will further amplify the cascading dissonance of lost expectations, and left unchecked will create a deep pool of apathy. (Pretty poetic musings, if I don't say so myself, which of course I did.)

These two aspects of shame, disappointment and being confounded, work in tandem and draw upon one another to create an ever increasing downward spiral. Confounded by the evidence of lost expectation creates a disappointment in self. This disappointment confounds, which produces more disappointment, and so on and so on. This cycle of self examination may be short or long, depending on the person and surrounding circumstances which will influence it also. To some people, this is how their entire life is conducted moving from one disappointment to another one, seemingly never able to break the cycle. But Jesus demonstrates the answer.

(25) Then he said unto them, O fools, and slow of heart to believe all that the prophets have spoken: (26) Ought not Christ to have suffered these things, and to enter into his glory? (27) And beginning at Moses and all the prophets, he expounded unto them in all the scriptures the things concerning himself.
— Luke 24:25-27

Jesus confronted their belief. They did not believe what the written evidence found in the Scriptures said about what the Messiah would be required to go through. Most of our disappointments come from a cursory belief of the matter before us rather than from a direct attack on a core belief. The enemy only comes at us from the place where we are weakest in our thinking. Consider that satan's question to the woman in the garden was directed to her about a command which she was not present to hear and required the man to relay it to her. Her core belief was not a direct revelation from the Father but a revelation experienced by another. Until she experienced it herself, any belief she had in it was susceptible to disappointment. The same still holds true with us.

Yet, in our text, Jesus begins to review with these disciples what the Scripture had already declared about Him. Being confounded by events which don't often appear accurate can only be corrected by examining the truth. A prophetic word spoken over an event does not typically provide all the details leading up to the event. Even many prophetic words cannot give every little detail or nuance which will play into the outcome, but they will give signposts that we need to look for. Many people get lost in the terrain of the prophetic and miss the signposts which are placed there to guide them through the journey. Confused and unable to distinguish the path, they look for one more prophetic word after another, hoping to find the path again, but all they keep getting are more signposts.

Notice how Jesus snapped them out of their stupor.

(28) And they drew nigh unto the village, whither they went: and he made as though he would have gone further. (29) But they constrained him, saying, Abide with us: for it is toward evening, and the day is far spent. And he went in to tarry with them.(30) And it came to pass, as he sat at meat with them, he took bread, and blessed it, and brake, and gave to them.(31) And their eyes were opened, and they knew him; and he vanished out of their sight. – Luke 24:28-31

Put yourself in the shoes of these disciples for a moment. Having experienced the disappointment of possibly missing a move of God in your life, your logic and reasoning are bombarded by truth straight from God himself, and yet you still don't understand. It's not until a practical application of a truth is administered that you finally can see the whole plan of God before you. The moment this happens, God hides Himself. He does this not to cause disappointment but to cause you to find Him anew.

In this passage, Jesus takes the bread, blesses it, breaks it, and gives it. To you and I in this and age, this might seem a very small thing, but it is monumental in the kingdom. These disciples had witnessed this act before, numerous times. If they were attendants at the final dinner which Jesus conducted merely three days prior, then they could recall the importance of the bread.

And he took bread, and gave thanks, and brake it, and gave unto them, saying, This is my body which is given for you: this do in remembrance of me. – Luke 22:19

Grace for Shame

Did they now understand that His body had to be broken open before everyone so the glory of the kingdom could be poured out? Did they finally recognize themselves in His actions to bring all men to the Father? Could they identify the principles of the kingdom of blessing, breaking and giving in their own life? Did they finally experience "grace for grace" for themselves? I would put before you that they didn't care about any of these things! God had just stepped into their life and solidified their belief in all that they had experienced with Jesus over three and half years through the simple act of sharing a meal.

I don't want you to think that eating is going to solve your disappointment. Many eating disorders already demonstrate that this is not the answer. In this example, it is the fellowship of people with a similar experience and expectation which brings back the flame of inspiration once snuffed in the vacuum of confusion. (Boy! Poetry twice in one chapter!) Paul tells us not to forsake the assembling of others for this very purpose. Disappointment is hard to disguise when you're with people who are going down or have been down the same path—unless everyone is disappointed with the path.

3.8 Despising Shame

*(1) Wherefore seeing we also are compassed about with so great a cloud of witnesses, let us lay aside every weight, and the sin which doth so easily beset us, and let us run with patience the race that is set before us, (2) Looking unto Jesus the author and finisher of our faith; who for the joy that was set before him endured the cross, **despising the shame**, and is set down at the right hand of the throne of God. – Hebrews 12:1-2*

These verses bring our study clearly into focus. We are each called to run a race in this life. Our success in this race is being watched by those who have gone before us. This is not a dash or wind sprint; it is a marathon. It requires patience not speed. Patience demands endurance.

Jesus is our model. He did it for us, because of us, and as us. Whatever you believe about the work that Jesus did, it is Him alone you start this belief from, and He is the one who your belief ends upon. At no point in this race which you are running are you relying upon any belief which you have in yourself to complete the contest. Your life doesn't exist in this race. This is the true measure of grace operating around you. Can people see you running, or do they *see* Jesus?

Jesus knew that despite what was required of Him there was a greater eternal reward which made the Father very happy. This was the joy that strengthened Him so He could endure the cross. Yet despite this joy, He had to confront shame head on.

In the two chapters where I've dealt with the purpose of the cross, I hope that I have conveyed to you what manner of shame Jesus was confronted with. I believe we see in the Garden of Gethsemane the victory Jesus had over shame as He prayed to the Father, "...not my will, but Thy will be done..." This is the model for all of our dealings with shame: allowing the Father's will to be done in our lives.

No one born into the world is automatically saved into the Kingdom of God. So until our conversion takes place, we navigate through the mind-fields of life (not mine-fields) trying to recognize the effects of our actions upon others. Shame, and the ensuing emotions, are some of the most devastating tools that we employ along this journey. In its use, shame, in an attempt to control, will create an environment inclined to repel and isolate. You avoid people who direct shame towards you and keep yourself a safe distance away from them.

Growing up though doesn't always provide us with the opportunity to keep shame from influencing us, especially through the people responsible for our health and well being. Multiple shame-venting attacks batter our self worth and often cripple relationships for years. Many come to despise their attacker. But what does that mean, "despise?"

According to *Webster's 9th Collegiate Dictionary*,

*"Despise may imply any emotional attitude ranging from indifferent **disdain** to **loathing**; **disdain** implies an arrogant or supercilious aversion to what is regarded as unworthily; **loathing** implies extreme disgust, detestation or hatred."*

Here comes the challenge: Once you're saved, religion tells you that you must love those very same people who you have come to despise! And the additional cross which you now have to bear is that you are to keep on loving them even as they continue to heap loads of shame upon you. Don't even consider for a moment forgetting these people; Jesus never forgot them! (Did you just notice that religion shamed you with Jesus! Welcome to the backhand of "What Would Jesus Do!")

What we have here is a failure to communicate. (I love this line!) In Hebrews 12:2, we see Jesus despised the shame – not the people who tried to put it upon him. I stated at the beginning of our focus on shame that shame is a social matter. It is a convention determining worth based upon a scale of comparison. It negates the individual value in order to impose the social value. Let me clarify this last statement: It takes away the value of Jesus in order to show the value of the rule of man.

Since man can only see his natural surroundings, any value he establishes is at best a fiat value since it does not include the spiritual value too. This partly explains Paul's statement to the Corinthians that had the princes of the age known what God proposed with Jesus, they would not have crucified Him. The true value of Jesus was much greater in the spiritual realm than what man could see.

The social value of shame is what Jesus despised on the cross. He was doing the will of the Father, but He was unwilling to identify Himself with the prevailing value system which did not fully recognize His true worth. At no point did He despise the people operating in that system, merely its efforts to control and dictate His purpose away from that of the Father's.

Yet we must remember this one thing: Jesus hung suspended between heaven and earth, caught between the tension of representing every man in His shame while seeing the reward beyond the cross, bringing many sons unto glory into the eternal plan of God. When He gave up His last breath, mankind, with all the social value which shame could collect, hung on that cross. In that moment, Jesus gave a picture of what the absolute wealth of the kingdom of darkness looked like for all who could see.

The total wealth of the Kingdom of God was displayed three days later when Jesus rose from the dead. In this act God validated all which Jesus had proclaimed about raising "the temple" on the third day. It confirmed that the kingdom of darkness, now bankrupt, had been overthrown by the Kingdom of God and that death no longer had any power over mankind. Now a kingdom established on grace was preeminent. This dominate expression of the King's actions will forever be recognized as the ultimate embarrassment to the rulers and principalities of darkness. Herein lies the value of the sacrifice – shame, embarrassment and humiliation have been exchanged to authorize us to function from a position of destined dominance.

Now comes the time for a decision on your part. It doesn't matter one bit whether you can claim that you have been saved or not. Knowingly or not, some facet of shame has tried to diminish the eternal value which God has placed upon you. God is saying to you, "Who said you are naked?"

Are you ready to accept the full measure of an exchange of grace? Before you answer this, you need to know what will be required of you. Realize that this is not a 12-step recovery program, where if you miss one thing, you start over again. It does not matter what you've experienced, so quit feeling obligated to tell me or anyone else what you've done or has been done to you. God knows, and that is enough. If you feel the pull to tell someone, just look in the mirror.

If you're dealing with feelings of not being worthy, you better know that you're not that important, because this reveals that you think what Jesus did was not sufficient to deal with your condition. Get over yourself. If that statement inflames you, then ask yourself this: Is it better that I get my significance from my emotions or from the Father? If your emotions win, then put this book down for a while. The Father will only draw near to you when you haven't placed something else higher than Him.

Every gift from the Kingdom of Grace is reciprocal in nature. You will be required to give it away once you receive it. This does not mean that you don't get to keep the result of receiving it; it still belongs to you. But out of the result you are to give to another. The abundant nature of the gift which you receive will continue to multiply to you only as long as you give away what you get. Your only requirement for giving is that you must give it all away joyfully.

So I'll ask again: Are you ready to accept the full measure of an exchange of grace? Are you willing to look upon the cross, seeing yourself and all of your shame there in Jesus, and pick up and put on your new identity as a son of God, completely void of any specter of shame? If so, then I want you to recognize that this is what it means to repent.

I know there is a lot of spiritual baggage associated with this term, and I've already defined its meaning. At the heart of it is a simple recognition of missing the mark which God placed before you to strive towards. Recall that the suffix "re" means to go back to the first occurrence or original. The word "pent" has a number of meanings, one being the high place, as in a *pent*house; and it also is the Greek term for the numerical value of five. Biblically, five signifies "grace." So "to repent" can mean to return to the high place of grace, which is the original intent of God for each of us.

If your heart tells you that it's time for you to repent, then say this out loud:

"Jesus, I take the gift you have given me. I divorce myself from the control of any shame which has affected my life. I nail that shame to the cross. I pick up and put on the full clothing of a son of God. Father, I thank you for taking my shame and dealing with it for me before all mankind. I boldly come to your Throne of Grace and assume my rightful position next to it with all the authority and power which being at such a place in your kingdom offers. I accept my new appointment as an ambassador of reconciliation in your Kingdom of Grace and agree to give that which has been given to me this day to all those who you place before me. As it is in Heaven, so let it be here in my life on Earth. So be it. Amen."

That is all it takes to begin. Now you have to walk it out. This means that you're going to cast down every thought which comes at you saying that you're not worthy. This will be your "despise" moment, and as you continue to do this, you will become stronger in the knowledge of what Jesus has done for you and the authority you have received through His actions.

Furthermore, with that simple prayer, you have received a kingdom promise found in Isaiah 61.

> *(6) But ye shall be named the Priests of the LORD: men shall call you the Ministers of our God: ye shall eat the riches of the Gentiles, and in their glory shall ye boast yourselves. (7) **For your shame ye shall have double**; and for confusion they shall rejoice in their portion: therefore in their land they shall possess the double: everlasting joy shall be unto them. (8) For I the LORD love judgment, I hate robbery for burnt offering; and I will direct their work in truth, and I will make an everlasting covenant with them. – Isaiah 61:6-8*

Verse 7 does not mean you will receive double shame, but it implies that you shall receive double *honor.* This is an important principle in the kingdom: Restoration never brings you back to where you were prior; it always causes at least a double increase. Whatever you have lost due to the effect of shame in your life, you are guaranteed at least a double return in honor before the very ones who inflicted the shame upon you.

Additionally, you are secured with a double portion in the land where you reside, which is able to assure you of everlasting joy. Recognize that this everlasting joy is the foundational component of the Kingdom of Grace. This means you will have the Kingdom of Grace forever reigning in your land.

Do you believe this? God will only provide to you what you believe in. If you believe that it is impossible for God to do this for you, great! This is the best way to get God to move on the matter, according to Luke.

> And he said, "The things which are impossible with men are possible with God." – Luke 18:27

If you're still not convinced, I guess you can continue to live as you have, getting the results you have always gotten. But is that any way to live in light of what you now know about the Kingdom of God? Yet God will not force His will upon you. So the decision is still up to you.

The Not-so-Subtle Aside

> Beloved, I wish above all things that you may prosper and be in health, even as your **soul** prospers. – 3 John 1:2

Shame, humiliation and embarrassment are soul issues. They comprise significant emotional events in each of our lives. For some, they are the epitome of a personal horror show; for others, each event represents just another shaky level in a house of cards. There is no easy way around this; these moments have been a vexing of your soul.

Yet God is concerned about all of you, not just your spiritual life, as is evident in this passage from 3 John. This passage connects your prosperity and health to the condition of your soul.

Okay, prosperity does not just mean money. Webster's declares it to be: *an advance or gain in anything good or desirable.* So consider this: Grace is your ability to experience the reciprocal giving nature of a loving Father—something which most would confess is a good or desirable thing. So in this capacity, grace could be considered as an ability to prosper. Yet, your ability to excel in this "grace-area" is directly related to how your soul is able to advance or gain in anything good or desirable.

Significant emotional events in the category we've been talking about can completely taint your ability to ever again see anything as being good or desirable. What is needed is an encounter which can break through the impact that these events have had on your life. The effect of this impact must be greater in intensity upon your soul than the intensity of all the shame you have experienced.

Remember the story I related a while back about Moses when he went up the mountain to speak to God and said that he wanted to see God's face. God told Moses that if was to see His face he would die, but that He would put him a cleft in the rock and cover him with His hand and permit Moses to see His back as His goodness passed by. This is the type of encounter that you need to have—a fresh look at the goodness of God.

I probably just lost a bunch of you there with this statement.

"I've been trying to find out what is that "ONE THING" that I need to do to get over this part of my life and this _____ (fill in the blank) just told me I need to encounter the goodness of God! I've been trying to do this at church for I don't know how long! Of all the sorry, worthless advice anyone could give me this takes the cake!! You have no idea what I've been through and what it has done to me. My life is a wreck, and I can't take it anymore!"

If I missed any points there, please feel free to fill them in. Yes, there is a point to my mentioning this story. When you look at someone face to face, each of you have the ability to see not only the person but where the person had just been, or what is more commonly known as their history. If you look at the back of a person, you see where they're headed, or what their future is.

In this story, God tells Moses that if he wants to look back at history, it will kill him. It would be the best choice to look to the future of where He was headed in order for him to receive His goodness.

Life is what happens between your past and your future. In other words, life is what happens now. Significant emotional events are your past. Living through life, repeatedly thinking of what if... if I could have, should have, would have... is to bring the past into your life of now. Once this is done you no longer live life; you relive that part of you which was mortified. And you keep killing your soul all over again.

Look, you've got this far reading this material, said a prayer which I trust made an adjustment in your perception, and maybe even had a tirade. So realize that I'm about to tell you something out of love which may seem at first pass as being heartless, but it will help in the long run. It is time for you to grow up into the things of God, and yes, this means that you need to have an encounter with Him.

Understand that Moses got to see the goodness of God by directing his eyesight to the future knowing God had prepared a place for him to see that goodness. This is another nature of grace:

Protect and cover to demonstrate greatness. God is prepared to do this with you too.

Your encounter will position you to receive all the provisions which God has stored up for your destiny. The abundant nature of His kingdom will overwhelm you and break off every limiting belief which your past has created, especially those beliefs about yourself.

Shame, embarrassment and humiliation place an identity upon us which is designed to keep God away. Moses killed an Egyptian while trying to set a Hebrew slave free. He had to carry that event around with him for over 40 years! It was the driving force of why he went into the desert, yet God intervened! He always does! This is what an encounter is about: allowing God to get you past yourself.

I cannot tell you how to have an encounter with God, simply because each encounter is a unique experience for every one of us. You have to just prepare yourself according to how the Lord leads you. Set aside a dedicated time to listen to His voice. Before you say you can't hear Him, please recognize that if He lives inside of you, He is going to sound just like you. It won't be some booming voice like James Earl Jones ("Luke, I am your father.") but a voice which you will easily recognize. Just follow what you hear, not discounting it as some "pizza dream." Your heart will know when it's God speaking or when it's your head speaking.

I'm also not saying that you only need one encounter. The Father alone knows the number of encounters that you require, but it is up to you to press for each and every one of them. The question is: How much desire do you have to see your soul prosper? I assure you that the Father has a greater desire for you to prosper than you even realize. The Father will not place more upon you than you can handle, but as I previously stated, it relies solely upon you to believe it.

There is one more thing which needs to be addressed in this entire subject. It has to do with why all of this matters. For this answer, you're going to have to read the next chapter.

3.9 Grace is about Relationships

There have been a number of topics which we've covered about grace, but in ending this study, I want to focus on the one primary function of grace: relationships. In order to express this properly, I want to bring to your attention a Scripture which I believe is the most perfect example of the environment of grace that you will ever witness in the entire Bible.

> The **grace** of the Lord Jesus Christ, and the **love** of God, and the **communion** of the Holy Ghost, be with you all. Amen.
> – 2 Corinthians 13:14

This passage is the closing to the last letter that Paul wrote to the church in Corinth. Some may see this as just a standard, if not noble, closing to a letter which at first glance would appear that way, yet Paul only used this closing here from all of the letters which he wrote. So I think the term "standard" doesn't truly fit the example. If you've just written an extensive letter to a body of people which commends them for their activities and faithfulness, wouldn't you want it to end on a high note, something which would hold their attention or bring it to remembrance at a later date? This is what we find here.

In this verse, we find a number of elements that describe the environment which fosters the presence of grace according to the Greek mind-set, yet we also see the fullness of the Godhead associated with those various aspects in this environment. While the term "environment" does portray the inner workings of a set area adequately, it is a rather harsh, stifling word, devoid of any real "life," and would probably work if I was writing this material for the scientific and research community. Since I'm not doing that, the more appropriate term would be captured in the word "relationship," and it is from here that we will delve into the heart of the matter.

What makes for good relationships?

There are a number of well written authors out there who can expound on what makes for a good relationship among any type of people group, yet it in this passage that we uncover the three aspects which are vital to every relationship. They are grace, love and communion. In the Greek, these are *charis*, **agapē** and **koinōnia**. The English rendition of these words belittles the synergy which they exhibit in the Greek culture, and it is my hope here that I will be able to bring this nature to life here for you. Since this is a study on grace, or *charis* in Greek, I'll leave this one for the last. So I'll start with love or **agapē** in the Greek.

Agapē

"Love," as the song goes, "is a many splendored thing." Paul associates love with God the Father, and John brings this out in the following passage.

(7) Beloved, let us love one another: for __love__ is of God; and every one that loveth is born of God, and knoweth God. (8) He that loveth not knoweth not God; for God is __love__. (9) In this was manifested the __love__ of God toward us, because that God sent his only begotten Son into the world, that we might live through

*him. (10) Herein is **love**, not that we loved God, but that he loved us, and sent his Son to be the propitiation for our sins. (11) Beloved, if God so loved us, we ought also to love one another. – 1 John 4:7-11*

In the Greek culture, they have several words which describe love, and many of their poets and philosophers wrote and expounded extensively on love shown to a brother or the love between a man and woman. Agapē never shared the limelight in these writings, and it wasn't until Paul, John, and the other New Testament writers began to incorporate it into their material that it began to receive any notoriety. Agapē came to represent the highest form of love which one could offer. Strong's Concordance defines agapē as, "*love*, that is, *affection* or *benevolence*; specifically (plural) a *love feast:* - (feast of) charity ([-ably]), dear, love." It is in this definition where we begin to uncover an element which represented the early church activities and sheds some light on part of Paul's first address to the Corinthians.

Love Feasts

In Acts 2, we come across the origin of what would later be called "love feasts."

*(42) And they continued steadfastly in the apostles' doctrine and fellowship, and in breaking of bread, and in prayers... (46) And they, continuing daily with one accord in the temple, and breaking bread from house to house, did eat their meat with gladness and singleness of heart, (47) Praising God, and having **favour** with all the people. And the Lord added to the church daily such as should be saved. – Acts 2:42, 46-47*

The daily breaking of bread from house to house is what we call today "the house church movement." It was the early believer's community structure which enabled them to pass along the apostle's doctrine and meet the needs of all that came under their influence. In the Greek language and culture, this feasting or eating together is what is known as agapē. Now I don't want you to get the idea that these were elaborate dinners with multitudes of different foodstuffs, because they often weren't at the beginning. They simply came together at the end of a busy day, bringing simple ingredients together, and they partook of the food which had been prepared. Bread and wine were integral elements since they represented the last supper of Jesus with His disciples.

What I find so interesting about these gatherings is that Saul used them to determine where the "church" was meeting and then subsequently persecuted the followers of Jesus before the religious leaders of the day. It was Saul's persecution of "love" which would force the church out of Jerusalem into the "world." The irony of all this is that Saul, who after his conversion became known as Paul, would provide direction in his first letter to the church at Corinth about how to conduct themselves during these agapē meals. They were following the extravagant manner of their past customs in conducting these feasts which left many who were not able to bring food hungry upon their completion. The corrections that Paul gave them would ultimately allow all the believers to experience the fullness of agapē in their community.

A crucial note in the history of these feasts occurred around 363-364 AD, when the Council of Laodicea passed an edict which forbade any church from celebrating an agapē feast. The feast during this time had become an evening supper of charity to the people attending where the sacraments would be offered to all as part of the meal. Even three hundred years later it would be addressed by the Quinsext Council of 692, and its practice would eventually disappear in the churches. I find it amazing that "the church" would outlaw the very cornerstone to its creation—the very symbol which, according to our opening passage, associates love to God. Why any church would think that it could practice its creed without the author of it is beyond me.

Koinōnia

Whenever people come together, whether it is at a meal or at a present-day church service, the one thing which you should be looking for is **koinōnia** or what we more commonly call fellowship. Another term that can be used here is "communion," and it possibly has the closest understanding to what **koinōnia** is trying to describe. Communion, or common union, indicates oneness in spirit, mind and communication. It is the essence of any lasting partnership. We have all had experiences where our communication with others has been "out of sorts," while at other times, it may have been "in sync." These instances demonstrate the effect that **koinōnia** has on our interaction with others.

The Holy Spirit is associated with **koinōnia** in Paul's passage, meaning that the Holy Spirit is the overseer of our fellowship with the Father. Jesus said that the Holy Spirit would be our Comforter, Counselor and Teacher, and that He would not speak on His own authority but that He would tell us of those things to come. These functions are vital to maintaining fellowship with the Father. Through the leading of the Holy Spirit, we are taught how to function correctly in God's Kingdom as a son and heir. The Holy Spirit will show us how to properly communicate and follow the protocol which the kingdom operates under so that we can remain in common union with both other believers and the Father. Our example in this would be as Jesus declared, where He only did those things which he saw the Father doing. There is an "oneness" that Jesus prayed for us to possess in John 17; this oneness is koinōnia.

Charis

You're at an event which exudes love among the participants, and there are obvious displays of affection and camaraderie. You are experiencing **agapē** and **koinōnia** in their fullest forms. As you experience this, you will start to witness the manifestation of *charis*, or grace, between the participants. I've already explored the foundational characteristic of grace in its nature of reciprocal giving, as well as its ability to produce joy. In the presence of **agapē** and **koinōnia**, *charis* raises to a whole new level which can best be categorized as "life-giving." If you've ever been a member of a group where whenever you met there was something which inspired you to be and give all that you could for "the cause," you have experienced the elevated effect of grace from a position of man. Take this to the level of the Kingdom of God, and it becomes personified as Jesus—the ultimate life-giving gift of God.

Paul clearly designates Jesus' work as the "grace-gift" in this relationship of the Godhead—a result of the love of the Father who seeks to bring communion with everyone through the Holy Spirit. If you take just one of these elements away, then the whole thing falls apart. Each of these three, *charis*, **agapē** and **koinōnia** are dependent upon and the result of their interaction with each other. Remove the elements of love, and people have no reason to extend a gift to another. Take away the fellowship, and there is no one to give to. And take away the joy of giving, and you end up with religion.

So in this one passage, we see the ultimate depiction of the relationship of the Godhead and how we are to mirror this same relationship one with another as a model of the Kingdom of God working in our lives. If we can ever get beyond the differences which we focus on and regain the sight of the purpose of the Father, we just might witness the power that comes from living a life of grace, the same power which the first church lived daily.

3.10 Dispeller of Shame

In finalizing the writing of this manuscript, believing that I had covered all the pertinent information, I was impressed to add this as the final insert. The title of this chapter conforms to the Hebrew understanding of the title of the book. More importantly it is the description of a name which can be traced back to a story of a rather important event wich stands as a prophetic marker in our kingdom destiny.

King David was a man after God's heart, so much so, that God rewarded him with an eternal kingdom, which is administrated by David's heir, and God's son, Jesus. This kingdom is where we operate from on this earth. When we look at the life of David, we see how a man sold out to God responds to the events in his life. His response demonstrated his expectation and reliance on the faithfulness of God's character to be displayed in his life. Many of you I recognize already know the background of David, so consider the first part of this to be a refresher course.

Before David was fully recognized as the King of Israel, he was a musician for the former King Saul. Saul's heir to the throne, Jonathan, took a great liking in David, and the two of them became friends. They pledged their love and loyalty to each other through a covenant. When King Saul became jealous of the fame which David gathered from the people of Israel, he attempted to imprison and kill David. Jonathan, aware of his father's intentions, warned David and helped him to hide. Then, he eventually helped to evade the patrols searching for him. Before parting each other's company they renewed their pledge to one another and to each of their families.

For many years, David lives as a fugitive on the run because of the desire of King Saul to see him killed. Never at any time did David attempt to kill the king in order to defend himself against the onslaught that he had to endure.

One day, during a great battle against the enemies of Israel, King Saul and Jonathan are killed, their bodies taken by the enemy, beheaded, and then hung from the walls of their city as a trophy. The inhabitants of Jabesh Gilead gathered their valiant men and traveled all night to retrieve the bodies and return them to Israel for a proper burial.

Dismayed at the loss of their king, Israel became torn about who should take over the position. The tribe of Judah crowned David as their king, while the remaining eleven tribes of Israel sought out one of the members from Saul's household to be their king. Over the course of the next seven years, David had skirmishes with the other king for the title of King of Israel. Eventually, a battle ensued which killed a majority of the men of importance in the northern kingdom, including those of Saul's household, and David was finally recognized throughout Israel as the one and only king.

Now we reach the point of this chapter. With all of his enemies subdued and peace in the land, David turned his heart to his lost friend and the promises which they had made to one another so many years ago. In Second Samuel, Chapter 9, we find the following story of David's fidelity to Jonathan.

> *(1) And David said, Is there yet any that is left of the house of Saul, that I may shew him kindness for Jonathan's sake?(2) And there was of the house of Saul a servant whose name was Ziba. And when they had called him unto David, the king said unto him, Art thou Ziba? And he said, Thy servant is he. (3) And the king said, Is there not yet any of the house of Saul, that I may shew the kindness of God unto him? And Ziba said unto the king, Jonathan hath yet a son, which is lame on his feet.*
> *– 2 Samuel 9:1-3*

The long cry of his heart and yearning of his soul was to find someone of Jonathan's family. It mattered not whether it was someone related to Jonathan or Saul. His love for his friend needed to be expressed properly. When a servant from Saul's house is found, he told King David that a child of Jonathan who is lame on his feet is alive.

The importance of his physical condition is vital to the overall story. You see when the child was five, he was in the care of a nurse, as would be common for a royal child. But during the time when he should be joyously playing in the safety of the palace, he was forced to flee for his life because of an uprising which was taking place. In the rush to leave with his nurse, he fell from the horse which would be his rescue and permanently injured his feet, causing his lameness. In this instance, he fell from royal prominence to a lifestyle marked by his lameness which all in Israel recognized as poverty. What a mighty blow to this young boy!

(4) And the king said unto him, Where is he? And Ziba said unto the king, Behold, he is in the house of Machir, the son of Ammiel, in Lodebar. (5) Then king David sent, and fetched him out of the house of Machir, the son of Ammiel, from Lodebar. – 2 Samuel 9:4-5

"Where is he?" Can you hear the cry of relief in this phrase? His physical condition is not important; in this cry, only his whereabouts mattered. I trust by now you know that Hebrew names matter in every description. Where is the heir of Jonathan staying? In the house of a salesman (Machir) for the people of God (Ammiel) in a pastureless land (Lodebar). Yet David sent word for the heir of Jonathan to be brought to him.

(6) Now when Mephibosheth, the son of Jonathan, the son of Saul, was come unto David, he fell on his face, and did reverence. And David said, Mephibosheth. And he answered, Behold thy servant! – 2 Samuel 9:6

The son of Jonathan, a lame young man, is brought before the King of Israel. How many times had he, the heir to the throne of the previous king, thought about this moment? He knew what the result of such a visit would produce: death. This was the reason why he had been rushed from the palace at such a young age. Yet any members who declared allegiance to the former king, and the welfare of his heirs were now dead. This young man recognized that having been discovered in the most obscure place in Israel, his impoverished life now was held in the hand of the King to do as he saw fit. "Behold thy servant!" is a plea for life more than a declaration of position.

Grace for Shame

(7) And David said unto him, Fear not: for I will surely shew thee kindness for Jonathan thy father's sake, and will restore thee all the land of Saul thy father; and thou shalt eat bread at my table continually. (8) And he bowed himself, and said, What is thy servant, that thou shouldest look upon such a dead dog as I am? (9) Then the king called to Ziba, Saul's servant, and said unto him, I have given unto thy master's son all that pertained to Saul and to all his house. (10) Thou therefore, and thy sons, and thy servants, shall till the land for him, and thou shalt bring in the fruits, that thy master's son may have food to eat: but Mephibosheth thy master's son shall eat bread alway at my table. Now Ziba had fifteen sons and twenty servants. (11) Then said Ziba unto the king, According to all that my lord the king hath commanded his servant, so shall thy servant do. As for Mephibosheth, said the king, he shall eat at my table, as one of the king's sons. – 2 Samuel 9:7-11

The King said, "Fear not."

Do not believe the imaginations in your heart. Do not hold onto images placed there by others who did not know the heart of the one you stand before.

Fear not. I know you better than you think, and I have a love for you that you know not of. Your physical condition has caused you take on an identity which I do not recognize as being who you truly are. Because I know your true worth, you shall have the heritage you lost in the fall returned to you.

Fear not. I have provided servants for you whose duty it is to work in your inheritance. They shall bring the harvest in for your posterity to feast upon so that they never have to beg as you have had to over these years since the fall.

Fear not. Whenever I take of the provision which God the Father has supplied to me, you will be there sharing with me from His goodness. Your true position of authority in this world shall be witnessed by everyone who eats with me since you will be there always as one of the King's sons.

Fear not, son of Jonathan. Today all shall know that the King does not see you as a lame, impoverished subject. On this day, son of Jonathan, your heritage shall no longer be viewed through the image of your physical condition or the folly of your grandfather, the first king of Israel. On this day, your destiny, defined in your very name, shall be made known throughout the kingdom. Fear not, Mephibosheth. Today you truly are the "dispeller of shame."

Closing

Many of you may feel like you're Jonathan's son—destined to do great things. However, somewhere along the way, a fall has fashioned a new identity in you, and it has situated you in a place, listening to someone sell you about what it's like to be a sheep in God's pasture, only to realize that pavement from the new parking lot ministry is not the covering that sheep truly need to thrive. Today, your King says, "Fear not! For I have dispelled all shame. Today, you are as one of the King's sons. Today, there is a throne you have access to which has always been your heritage. Your past, present and future were already dealt with in the compassion displayed in the work of my Son. There is nothing left for you to do but rejoice. And again I say rejoice."

There is only one thing that can be said now.

Peace and Grace to You,

Mike

About the Author

Mike and his family live in Portland, Oregon, where he is one of the teachers of the Word of God at International Life Center in Clackamas, Oregon. As a graduate of the Latin University of Theology, Mike is passionate about people understanding what the purpose of grace is in their lives and how it changes communities that are determined to operate from its authority. Mike contributes his insights about the world of grace at www.graceforshame.com and www.mygrace2u.com.

Reflections

_____

_____

_____

_____

_____

_____

_____

_____

_____

_____

_____

_____

_____

_____

_____

_____

_____

_____

_____

_____

_____

_____

_____

_____

_____

_____

_____

_____

_____

_____

_____